Quick Guide to Local Birds

This guide is organized by families so related species are shown together, with a few birds found primarily in the mountains grouped at the end. The Species Account pages are color-coded and thumb-indexed in the following manner:

WATERFOWL (Geese, Swans, Dabbling Ducks)

WATERFOWL (Diving Ducks)

UPLAND GAME BIRDS (Quail, Pheasant, Grouse) – LOONS – GREBES – CORMORANTS – WADING BIRDS (Bittern, Herons)

VULTURE – EAGLE AND HAWKS – RAIL AND COOT

SHOREBIRDS (Plovers, Oystercatcher, Sandpipers, Whimbrel, Turnstone, Dowitchers, Snipe, Phalarope)

GULLS AND TERNS – ALCIDS (Murre, Guillemot, Murrelet, Auklet)

PIGEONS AND DOVES – OWLS – NIGHTHAWK – SWIFTS

HUMMINGBIRDS – KINGFISHER – WOODPECKERS – FALCONS (Kestrel, Merlin, Peregrine) – FLYCATCHERS (Wood-Pewee, Flycatchers, Kingbirds)

SHRIKE – VIREOS – CORVIDS (Jays, Crow, Raven) – SWALLOWS (Martin, Swallows)

CHICKADEES – BUSHTIT – NUTHATCH – CREEPER – WRENS – DIPPER – KINGLETS – THRUSHES (Bluebird, Thrushes, Robin)

STARLING – PIPIT – WAXWING – WARBLERS

NATIVE SPARROWS (Towhee, Sparrows, Junco) – WESTERN TANAGER – BLACK-HEADED GROSBEAK

BLACKBIRDS (Blackbirds, Meadowlark, Cowbird, Oriole) – FINCHES (Finches, Crossbill, Siskin, Evening Grosbeak) – HOUSE SPARROW

MOUNTAIN SPECIALTIES

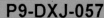

P9-DXJ-057

BIRDS OF THE PUGET SOUND REGION

By

Bob Morse
Tom Aversa
Hal Opperman

R.W. Morse Company
Olympia, Washington

For My Grandchildren (B.M.)

For Cheryl (T.A.)

For JoLynn (H.O.)

Published by the R.W. Morse Company, Olympia, Washington
Copyright ©2003 by the R.W. Morse Company

Library of Congress Control Number: 2003092423
EAN 9780964081024   **$19.95 Softcover**
First Edition 2003
Twelth Printing 2013 (updated)

Printed by
Imago

Authors
Bob Morse, Tom Aversa, and Hal Opperman

Editor
Hal Opperman

Cover and Interior Design
Gina Calle

Map
Shawn K. Morse

Bird Drawings
Eric Kraig

Cover Photograph of Rufous Hummingbird
William Zittrich

Contents

Common Local Birds

Here are some of the most common birds in the Puget Sound Region. For more information about each bird, go to its Species Account.

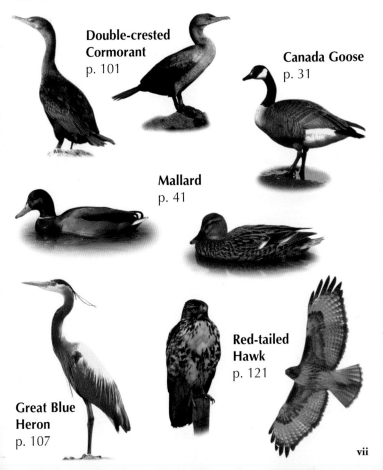

Double-crested Cormorant
p. 101

Canada Goose
p. 31

Mallard
p. 41

Great Blue Heron
p. 107

Red-tailed Hawk
p. 121

Glaucous-winged Gull
p. 173

American Crow
p. 257

Rock Pigeon
p. 187

Northern Flicker
p. 223

Rufous Hummingbird
p. 213

Steller's Jay
p. 255

Violet-green Swallow
p. 265

Downy Woodpecker
p. 219

Barn Swallow
p. 271

Chestnut-backed Chickadee p. 275

Black-capped Chickadee p. 273

Red-breasted Nuthatch p. 279

Bushtit p. 277

Bewick's Wren p. 289

American Robin p. 303

Spotted Towhee p. 329

European Starling p. 307

Song Sparrow p. 337

House Finch p. 363

Dark-eyed Junco p. 345

Red-winged Blackbird p. 351

American Goldfinch p. 369

Pine Siskin p. 367

House Sparrow p. 373

Introduction

Bird watching, or birding, has become one of America's most popular outdoor activities. It is estimated that one-fifth of all Americans – 46 million people – either watch or feed birds. Birding can be great family entertainment. It is easy to get started, inexpensive, healthy, and allows us to understand and appreciate the natural world.

Given the popularity of bird watching and the beauty of the Pacific Northwest, it is little wonder that the people of the Puget Sound Region enjoy seeing and studying our local birds. The Region has a rich variety of bird life with over 200 species of birds that are permanent residents or regular annual visitors to the 12 counties surrounding Puget Sound. These are the birds featured in this guide. Those that can readily be found in the lowlands receive full Species Accounts. An additional 12 species likely to be encountered at higher elevations of the Cascade and Olympic Mountains are illustrated and briefly discussed in a special section on Mountain Specialties.

Birds of the Puget Sound Region is for beginning bird watchers who wish to identify the birds of the greater Puget Sound area. This guide will also appeal to experienced birders who wish to learn more about the behavior, habitats, and seasonal occurrence of our local birds.

Our web site, at www.rwmorse.com, provides a synopsis of the guide and a method for ordering copies of the book. We openly solicit suggestions to make the guide more accurate and complete. Please send these to Bob Morse at rwmorse@comcast.net.

GEOGRAPHICAL COVERAGE

Birds of the Puget Sound Region is centered on the inland marine waters of Washington, including the eastern part of the

Strait of Juan de Fuca, the southern end of the Strait of Georgia at the U.S.-Canada border, Puget Sound proper down to Tacoma and Olympia, Hood Canal, and the many connecting bays, inlets, and passages. The term "Region", as used in the guide, refers to this entire geographical area, as depicted on the map inside the front cover. The land portions of the Region are those that drain toward the Sound, from sea level up to the crest of the Olympic Mountains and the Cascade Range, embracing 12 counties: King, Pierce, Snohomish, Kitsap, Thurston, Whatcom, Skagit, Island, Mason, San Juan, and the eastern half of Clallam and Jefferson. This book is for anyone interested in bird life in or near Seattle, Tacoma, Everett, Bellingham, Olympia, Bremerton, Mount Vernon, Port Angeles, Port Townsend, and Shelton.

CONSERVATION

Increased development of the Puget Sound Region's urban and rural communities has led to changes in habitat and habitat loss, impacting our local bird populations. Pollution of Puget Sound waters by farms, pulp mills, sewage, marinas, garbage dumps, and storm runoff has had a direct effect on the Region's waterbirds. Some populations have seen declines of up to 80 percent over the last 20 years. Deforestation has also taken its toll, as has urban and suburban sprawl. A diverse and thriving bird life is an excellent indicator of a healthy environment. Those who enjoy birds should do all they can to protect birds and their habitats. We urge you to join one of the many conservation organizations such as local Audubon chapters, People for Puget Sound, the Washington Wilderness Coalition, the Washington Environmental Council, or The Nature Conservancy of Washington, that strive to address and improve environmental conditions.

Identifying Birds

It can be confusing when you first start trying to identify birds. First, look at the general shape, size, and color of the bird. Check the Common Local Birds (pages vii–x) and see if it is there. If not, scan through the Species Account pages for your bird. Read the description – especially the **boldfaced** text – to see how it matches your bird. Compare range, similar species, and habitat. Keep comparing the bird to the book until you have a match.

The different colors of a bird's feathering ("plumage") and bare parts (bill, legs, feet) provide one of the best ways to identify a bird. Most of the plumages and color patterns for each bird species are unique. However, plumages may vary within the same species between the sexes, between adults and younger birds, and by season.

In some species the male and the female have distinctly different plumages. Good examples are Mallard, House Finch, Red-winged Blackbird, and Rufous Hummingbird. Usually the males have the most brilliant colors, as in these examples, while the females have muted colors so they are not easily detected as they incubate eggs and raise young. Other species such as Rock Pigeon, Steller's Jay, American Crow, and Song Sparrow show no plumage differences between the sexes.

Most birds seen in the Puget Sound Region in spring and summer display what is known as their summer or "breeding" plumage. Birds seen here in winter are usually in their "non-breeding" or winter plumage. Typically, but not always, the breeding plumage is more colorful or highly patterned and the non-breeding plumage is more muted.

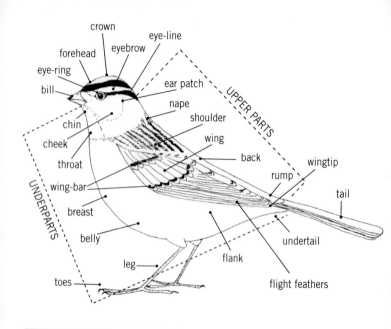

Parts of a Bird. It is helpful to know the names of the different parts of a bird. These sketches of a White-crowned Sparrow and an in-flight Mallard show the terms used to describe bird anatomy in this guide.

Molting is the process of replacing worn feathers with new, fresh feathers. Most local birds replace some or all of their feathers in a molt in summer or early fall when they change into their non-breeding plumage. Most birds molt again in late winter or spring as they change into their breeding plumage. These molts occur over a period of several weeks or months.

Some birds have different plumages as they mature. This is particularly true for gulls, which take up to four years and

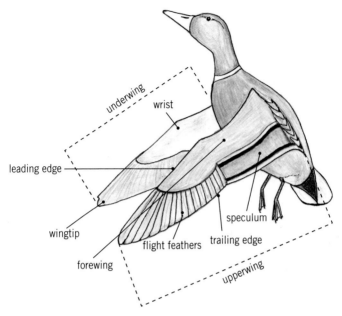

underwing

wrist

leading edge

wingtip

speculum

flight feathers   trailing edge

forewing

upperwing

several plumage stages to gain their adult plumage.

The term "juvenal plumage" refers to the plumage of a new-born bird after it loses its initial downy feathers. Some species hold this plumage for only a few weeks after fledging while others may hold it into winter. "First-year plumage" is used for the plumage during the first 12 months of a bird's life. "Immature" refers to all plumages before the bird gains its adult plumage.

Colors and patterning may vary considerably among birds of the same species and plumage stage, especially when they belong to different geographical populations. For instance, the Fox Sparrows that nest in the Cascades differ markedly in appearance from the ones that arrive to spend the winter in the lowlands of the Puget Sound Region. Differences can be great even within the same local population. In our Region the majority of Red-tailed Hawks have light breasts and underwings, yet a certain percentage of birds have dark-brown underparts and dark underwings with lighter-colored flight feathers. Such consistently different types are called "color morphs" (or just morphs).

In this book the birds are presented in family groupings, as shown in the Quick Guide to Local Birds on the first page inside the front cover. Beginning birders will find that learning the characteristics of the different bird families will make bird identification both easier and quicker. Birds in the same family look similar and often behave in a similar manner. Hummingbirds, for example, are all small, with long, thin bills, have fast wing-beats, and can hover. Once you see a bird with these characteristics, you are well on your way to identifying it as a hummingbird.

Don't expect every bird you see to look exactly like the photographs in this guide. Birds, like people, are individuals. To appreciate how variable birds of the same species can be, study the ones that come regularly to your backyard feeder. Male House Finches, for example, can show a wide range of coloration from rich, deep red to golden yellow. You may find that, with practice, you can learn to recognize individual birds by the subtle differences in their markings.

Binoculars

Binoculars are a great help in getting good views of birds. Binoculars come in many sizes. Each is labeled with two numbers, e.g., 7 x 35, 8 x 40, 10 x 50. The first number is the magnification. You may think that the larger the magnification, the better the binocular. However, as magnification increases, clarity may diminish as well as field of view (the width of the area you can see at a given distance). Another trade-off is that the higher-powered binoculars are usually heavier, hence harder to hold steady or carry for extended periods of time.

The second number is the diameter of the big lens (objective) in millimeters. The larger the diameter, the greater the light-gathering capability of the binocular and the more colors and details you can see, especially in poor light conditions.

Many discount stores offer binoculars in the $50 to $100 price range, which may be suitable for beginning birders. Higher-quality binoculars are available at nature stores or camera shops and can cost from $1500 to $2500.

The best way to select a binocular is to go to a store that has good selection and try out several. If you wear glasses, fold, screw, or snap down the eyecups to get your pupil closer to the lens so you get a larger image. Look at a sign at the other end of the store and see which binocular provides the sharpest image. There should be no distortion in either shape or color. Which one feels more comfortable in the hand? Is it easy to change focus? Can you focus on close objects (within 10–15 feet)? Which is the most durable and has the largest field of view?

Out in the field, examine what other birders are using and ask for the opportunity to look through their binoculars. Selecting a binocular is a personal thing – what is comfortable for you may not be for another birder. So, choose one that has sufficient magnification (7 or 8 power), a wide objective lens (40 mm or more), an acceptable field of view (300 feet or more at 1000 yards), is easy to use, and fits your budget. A good rule of thumb is to buy the best binocular you can afford.

Also, make sure you get a wide binocular strap (at least one inch). It will help prevent a sore neck by the end of the day. Even better are some of the harnesses that transfer binocular weight to the shoulders rather than the neck. Binoculars also come with dust covers for each of the four lenses. Better-quality binoculars are waterproof, but in the Puget Sound Region it is nonetheless a good idea to purchase a removable rain guard to cover the small eyepieces so you do not have to wipe them dry all the time.

Finally, take time to pre-focus your binocular before using it. Do this by adjusting the central focus knob and the eyepiece focus until the image appears sharp through both lenses.

Attracting Birds to Your Yard

Most people get involved in bird watching by observing the birds that appear in their yards. Perhaps the easiest way to see birds is to put up feeders and watch for birds to appear. When they are perched and eating, birds tend to stay long enough for you to study the field marks at close range and identify the bird.

Although just hanging out a birdseed feeder will attract some birds, a complete backyard bird program has three important requirements: **food**, **water**, and **shelter**. By careful attention to all three of these elements you will not only increase the number and variety of birds that visit your yard, but you will also be contributing to their wellbeing. Many helpful books and brochures on bird feeding, nest boxes, and gardening for wildlife are available at nature stores and nurseries.

FOOD

The food that birds eat comes mainly from natural sources. Native and ornamental shrubs, trees, and other plants provide fruits, seeds, flowers, and insects. You will attract more birds to your yard by selecting plants favorable to birds.

You may also provide seed, suet, and other products to entice birds to your yard. Many seeds are suitable for feeding birds although the best product in the Puget Sound Region is black-oil sunflower seed, which has high fat content. Many grocery and hardware stores sell a birdseed mix that contains some black-oil sunflower seed but often has a lot of millet (the small, round, tan-colored seed) and filler grains. When you place this seed in a hanging feeder five to six feet off the ground, some of the birds will eat only the sunflower seed and kick the filler and millet to the ground. In elevated feeders, it is much better to use only black-oil sunflower seed or a specialized mix that is high in nutritional value.

Different birds have different feeding preferences. You may wish to try more than one of the following common feeder types, depending on the species of birds you wish to attract.

- **Fly-through and hopper feeders** are hung or mounted on a pole or deck normally five to six feet above the ground. Stocked with black-oil sunflower seed, they attract Steller's Jay, finches, Red-breasted Nuthatch, and chickadees.

- A **ground feeder or platform feeder** is placed near the ground or up to table height and filled with millet, corn, or a birdseed mix that has some black-oil sunflower seeds but is mostly millet. This feeder will attract doves, pigeons, ducks, sparrows, Dark-eyed Junco, Spotted Towhee, and Red-winged Blackbird. Buy a ground feeder with a bottom screen that allows the rain to drain through.

- Cylindrical **tube feeders** are either hung or mounted and can be filled with a nutritional mix of birdseed or just black-oil sunflower seed. They attract the smaller birds such as Red-breasted Nuthatch, Pine Siskin, chickadees, and finches.

- A specialized tube feeder to hold niger thistle seed is called a **thistle** or **finch feeder** and can attract numbers of finches like House Finch, Pine Siskin, and American Goldfinch.

- **Suet**, either acquired at a local meat market or purchased at the nature store in suet cakes, attracts woodpeckers, Red-breasted Nuthatch, chickadees, Bushtit, and a host of other birds seeking its high-energy fat.

- Red **hummingbird feeders** attract Rufous and Anna's Hummingbirds that breed in the Puget Sound Region. It is easy to make hummingbird nectar: mix one part sugar to four parts water, boil, let cool, and then fill your feeders. Do not add any artificial food coloring; the red of the feeder is sufficient to attract hummingbirds.

Experiment with your feeder locations and different birdseed to learn what works best in your yard. Feeders should be placed close to natural shelters such as bushes and trees so the birds can escape from predators. You can feed the birds all year long without worrying that your bird feeding will delay the birds' fall migration. They will leave when the time is right.

WATER

Birds need water for bathing and drinking. You will find that you attract more birds if you offer a reliable source of clean water in your yard. Consider placing a concrete birdbath filled with one inch of water to meet their needs. Clean and refill it regularly. Be sure the bottom surface is rough so the birds can get a good footing. Place the birdbath near shrubs or trees where they can preen after bathing and escape from predators. Try adding a dripper to the birdbath. The sound of dripping water attracts birds.

SHELTER AND NEST BOXES

Birds need cover so they can seek protection from bad weather and predators. Nearby bushes, shrubs, and trees will help meet their needs as will a loosely-stacked brush pile. Neighborhood cats can be a real problem, especially when they lurk beneath feeders and birdbaths. Careful placement or screening off of feeders and birdbaths, or placing chicken wire strategically in front of favorite cat stalking areas, will help protect the birds.

Some of the birds featured in this guide are cavity-nesters and may be enticed to use a bird house which you can either build yourself or purchase at a nature store. It is important to realize that there is no such thing as a generic nest box. Different birds have different needs, and each nest box has to meet the demands of its occupant or it will not be used. The size of the opening and its height above the floor are critical, as is the height of the nest box above the ground. Some nest boxes also serve as wintering roosting boxes for the smaller birds. It may take a season or two to attract chickadees, nuthatches, or swallows to your nest boxes. Once they start nesting on your property, you will enjoy watching the behavior of these nesting birds.

HYGIENE

Feeders, the ground below the feeders, and birdbaths need to be cleaned on a regular basis to eliminate the possibility of the spread of avian diseases. Scrub the feeders and birdbaths with soap and water. Mix one part bleach to ten parts hot water to sanitize them. Rinse them well then let them dry completely before refilling.

Be sure to inspect nest boxes each fall and give them a good cleaning, but use no insecticides. Discard used nesting materials. Repair any damage so the boxes are ready and waiting for their new occupants to arrive in spring.

Observing Birds

Many bird watchers are quite content just to watch the birds in their yards casually. Some, however, get more involved and begin to look for birds beyond their immediate neighborhood. To get the most out of birding in the field, look, listen, and move slowly. Try to keep conversations to a minimum.

To help locate birds, watch for their movement and listen for their calls. Most often we see birds fly to a nearby branch or flit around in a tree. Their movement catches our attention. But an important part of bird watching is listening and, many times, it is its song or call that draws us to the bird.

Bird songs are a good way to identify birds. Each bird species has a unique song, and, with practice, you can learn to differentiate the songs. You can purchase tapes or CDs that allow you to study bird vocalizations at your leisure. With experience, you will be able to identify birds simply by their songs and calls.

WHEN TO GO BIRDING

Small birds tend to be most active when they are feeding early in the morning (as early as daybreak). Shorebirds tend be most active while they are feeding on incoming and outgoing tides; they often rest at high tides. Hawks become active in the morning after the rising temperature creates thermals that allow them to soar through the air. Most owls are nocturnal and are most active in the evening or just before dawn.

Puget Sound birds vary with the season. If you go out in different seasons, you may see different birds. Some species stay in the Region throughout the year while others arrive in the spring and leave in the fall. Other species migrate into the lowlands of our area from the north, the mountains, or the interior of the continent and spend the winter.

Spring is a great time of year. The flowers are blossoming, the trees are getting their buds, and the birds, in their bright breeding plumages, return from their wintering grounds. The males start singing and the local nesting birds seek mates, breed, and start to raise their families. Hummingbirds feed on flower nectar or at feeders. Wintering birds head north to their breeding grounds.

In summer, the local young birds hatch, and their parents are busy feeding them. As summer progresses, the young learn to fly and fend for themselves. By August, summer visitors are beginning to head south for their wintering grounds.

By late fall, the last Arctic-breeding shorebirds have passed through on their way south. As fall changes to winter, flocks of waterfowl appear on our lakes and ponds. Dunlins arrive to winter on local mudflats. Our resident birds continue to use neighborhood bird feeders, joined by winter visitors driven down to the lowlands by snowfall in the mountains.

KEEPING RECORDS

Some people keep a checklist of all the birds that appear in their yard ("yard list") or of all the birds seen in their lifetime ("life list"). As lists grow, so does a sense of personal accomplishment. Along with the pleasure of finding new and different birds comes an incentive to learn more about them. Many dedicated bird watchers keep a detailed journal of what they see, when and where, and the bird's behavior. Careful record keeping by knowledgeable observers can contribute greatly to scientific understanding of bird life.

A checklist of the local birds is provided on pages 385-389.

Bird Habitats in the Puget Sound Region

The place where a bird or other living creature is normally found is termed its "habitat". Birds are quite diverse in their habitat requirements. Brown Creepers are seldom seen over open salt water or loons in trees. To a large extent, the secret to finding and identifying birds is knowing the habitats and developing an understanding of which birds are likely to be seen where. The more types of habitat you explore, the greater the variety of birds you will see.

The Puget Sound Region has eleven major habitat categories:

OPEN SALT WATER

This habitat includes all the salt waters of Puget Sound and adjoining inlets, bays, and straits including the Strait of Juan de Fuca and the Strait of Georgia. Open salt water is host to loons, grebes, cormorants, scaups, scoters, goldeneyes, gulls, terns, and alcids. Purple Martins nest locally in a few saltwater bays. There are many vantage points to scan saltwater habitats including Discovery Park, Point Defiance Park, Semiahmoo Spit, Dosewallips State Park, Point Wilson, Point No Point, and John Wayne Marina.

ROCKY SHORE

The rocky shore habitat includes cobbled beaches, breakwaters, and rocky outcroppings along the saltwater shoreline. Alki Point, Ediz Hook, Deception Pass, and Penn Cove attract a selection of birds that prefer this habitat, including cormorants, Black Oystercatcher, turnstones, and Surfbird, while Harlequin Ducks tend to feed in the waters off these shores.

SANDY SHORE, MUDFLATS, AND SALT MARSH

The extensive mudflats of the Nisqually National Wildlife Refuge, the Stanwood area, and Kennedy Creek offer feeding habitat for migrating and wintering shorebirds, while Padilla Bay's mudflats provide food for large numbers of wintering waterfowl. Sandy shores often host numbers of shorebirds and gulls. Salt marshes may host Great Blue Heron, Virginia Rail, ducks, and shorebirds.

FRESH WATER, MARSH, AND SHORE

Lake Washington, Lake Sammamish, and American Lake are just some of the many freshwater areas that abound in the Puget Sound Region. Great Blue Heron, Bald Eagle, Osprey, and Belted Kingfisher obtain fish from these waters, and waterbirds such as grebes, geese, ducks, and coots may be found there. American Bittern, Green Heron, and Virginia Rail skulk in marsh vegetation. Cattails often support nesting Marsh Wrens and Red-winged Blackbirds. Swallows catch insects over the water, while songbirds such as Yellow Warbler frequent the trees and bushes along the water's edges, foraging for food.

WET CONIFEROUS FOREST

This habitat includes coniferous forests at low and middle elevations, dominated by Douglas-fir, western hemlock, and western redcedar. These woods are home to Band-tailed Pigeon, a few owls, Hairy Woodpecker, Hammond's Flycatcher, Steller's Jay, Chestnut-backed Chickadee, Pacific Wren, Golden-crowned Kinglet, Varied Thrush, Western Tanager, Yellow-rumped Warbler, and Pine Siskin. At higher elevations, forests of silver fir, mountain hemlock, and subalpine fir host Sooty Grouse, Gray Jay, Hermit Thrush, and Townsend's Warbler.

BROADLEAF FOREST

This habitat includes stands of red alder, black cottonwood, bigleaf and vine maple, and madrone. Extensive broadleaf woodlands line the riparian zone along many creeks and larger streams throughout the Puget Sound Region – as in the Skagit, Dungeness, Snoqualmie, and Stillaguamish River valleys. Broadleaf trees often grow in mixed stands with conifers as well as in uniform stands after the logging of coniferous forests. The birds that prefer this habitat include Ruffed Grouse, Western Screech- and Barred Owls, Red-breasted Sapsucker, Downy Woodpecker, Western Wood-Pewee, Pacific-slope Flycatcher, Hutton's, Warbling, and Red-eyed Vireos, Black-capped Chickadee, and Black-throated Gray and Wilson's Warblers.

OAK PRAIRIES

This small, threatened lowland habitat occurs in some of the driest parts of the Puget Sound Region, such as the San Juan Islands in the rain shadow of the Olympic Mountains. It is characterized by native grasslands and scattered stands of garry oak. The most extensive remaining examples are the South Sound Prairies that dot the fast-draining, gravelly soils extending from Fort Lewis west to Tenino and Littlerock. Birds to be found in such places include California Quail, Common Nighthawk, House Wren, Western Bluebird, Chipping Sparrow, and Western Meadowlark.

SUBALPINE PARKLAND AND ALPINE MEADOWS

This high-elevation, open habitat of the Cascades and Olympics consists of meadows with alpine wildflowers and scattered stands of trees. Look here for White-tailed Ptarmigan, Horned Lark, Mountain Bluebird, American Pipit, and Gray-crowned Rosy-Finch. Paradise and Sunrise at Mount Rainier National Park, Hurricane Ridge and Deer Park in Olympic National Park, Mount Baker, and the North Cascades Highway offer good access to this habitat.

SHRUBBY THICKETS

Shrubby thickets exist in clearings and around the edges of coniferous and broadleaf woods, transportation and power-line corridors, and overgrown fencerows. Willow Flycatcher, Bushtit, Bewick's Wren, Orange-crowned and MacGillivray's Warblers, Spotted Towhee, and sparrows live in this habitat.

PARKS AND GARDENS

This urban and suburban habitat attracts many of the birds that come to our backyard bird feeders, including hummingbirds, woodpeckers, chickadees, Red-breasted Nuthatch, grosbeaks, Purple and House Finches, and American Goldfinch. This habitat also hosts Rock Pigeon, American Crow, American Robin, European Starling, and House Sparrow.

FARMLAND AND PASTURES

The open pastures and agricultural fields of the lowlands host Northern Harrier, Ring-necked Pheasant, Mourning Dove, Short-eared Owl, and many wintering geese, swans, ducks, hawks, eagles, falcons, gulls, starlings, and blackbirds. Prime examples of farmlands include the Snoqualmie Valley and the Skagit, Samish, and Lummi Flats.

Birding Around Puget Sound

One of the best ways to see new birds is to join the local Audubon Society on a field trip. Participants often visit new areas, learn how to identify new birds, and meet people who share a common interest.

After studying the birds in your yard, visit local parks and greenbelts. A selection of top birding locations of the Puget Sound Region is listed below, arranged by counties. For maps and directions to these and other fine Regional birding sites, consult the birdfinding guides listed on pages 21–22 and the Audubon chapter web sites referenced on page 22.

Clallam Ediz Hook, Dungeness Spit, Dungeness River, Sequim Bay/John Wayne Marina, Olympic National Park (Hurricane Ridge, Deer Park), Diamond Point

Island Crockett Lake, Penn Cove, Admiralty Inlet, Libbey Beach County Park, Deception Pass State Park, Camano Island, Deer Lagoon

Jefferson Port Townsend (Fort Worden, Point Wilson), Marrowstone Island (Fort Flagler State Park), Port Townsend-Coupevile ferry, Protection Island, Quilcene Bay, Dosewallips State Park, Mount Walker

King Discovery Park, Green Lake, Juanita Bay, Montlake Fill/Union Bay, Alki Point, Snoqualmie Valley, Stevens Pass, Snoqualmie Pass, Dash Point State Park, Lake Sammamish State Park, Marymoor Park

Kitsap Point No Point, Foulweather Bluff Preserve, Rich Passage, Fort Ward State Park, Edmonds-Kingston ferry

Mason Hood Canal, Theler Wetland, Kennedy Creek

Pierce Mount Rainier National Park (Sunrise, Paradise), Joint Base Lewis-McChord, American Lake, Gog-Le-Hi-Te Wetland/Puyallup River mouth, Tacoma waterfront (Ruston Way), Point Defiance Park/Tacoma Narrows

San Juan Orcas Island (Moran State Park/Mount Constitution), San Juan Island (English Camp, American Camp, Cattle Point), inter-island ferry

Skagit Samish Flats, Skagit Flats, Fir Island (Skagit Wildlife Area), Padilla Bay, Anacortes (Washington Park), North Cascades Highway

Snohomish Spencer Island, Stanwood area, Darrington area, Everett sewage ponds, Everett waterfront, Edmonds fishing pier, Crescent Lake Wildlife Area

Thurston Watershed Park (Olympia), Nisqually National Wildlife Refuge, Capitol State Forest/Black Hills, Budd Inlet/Olympia waterfront, Black Lake Meadows, Scatter Creek Wildlife Area, Mima Mounds

Whatcom Birch Bay, Semiahmoo Spit, Blaine Marine Park, Lummi Flats, Larrabee State Park, Tennant Lake (Ferndale), North Cascades Highway, Mount Baker

Helpful Resources

There are a number of ways to get additional information about birds and their habitats, bird identification, and good places to go birding. Some of the best information is available through books, birding organizations, web sites, and local nature stores. Here are some of our favorites:

REGIONAL PUBLICATIONS

Hal Opperman. 2003. *A Birder's Guide to Washington*. With contributions from members of the Washington Ornithological Society. Colorado Springs: American Birding Association. Includes maps, descriptions for close to 250 birding sites in Region, species accounts, seasonal abundance graphs.

The Great Washington State Birding Trail: Cascade Loop (2002), *Southwest Loop (2005), Olympic Loop (2007), and Puget Loop (2012)*. Olympia, Washington: Audubon Washington. Large folding maps, descriptions of over 100 birding sites in the Puget Sound Region.

Eugene S. Hunn. 2012. *Birding in Seattle and King County*, rev. ed. Seattle Audubon Society. Abundance, geographical distribution of birds; graphs of seasonal status; dozens of birding routes discussed, mapped.

Mark G. Lewis and Fred A. Sharpe. 1987. *Birding in the San Juan Islands*. Seattle: The Mountaineers. Full accounts of species present in archipelago; when and where to find them.

Terence R. Wahl. 1995. *Birds of Whatcom County Status and Distribution*. Bellingham, Washington: The Author. Species accounts; valuable discussions of habitats, historical changes.

Philip H. Zalesky. 2001. *Birding in Snohomish County*, rev. ed. Everett, Washington: Pilchuck Audubon Society. Good selection of birding sites, with maps.

Arthur R. Kruckeberg. 1991. *The Natural History of Puget Sound Country*. Seattle and London: University of Washington Press. Superb introduction to topography, climate, plant and animal life, human impact on Region. Lavishly illustrated.

IDENTIFICATION GUIDES

David Allen Sibley. 2003. *The Sibley Field Guide to Birds of Western North America*. New York: Alfred A. Knopf.

Jon L. Dunn and Jonathan Alderfer. *Field Guide to the Birds of North America,* Sixth Edition. 2011. Washington, D. C.: National Geographic Society.

Kenn Kaufman. 2005. *Kaufman Field Guide to Birds of North America*. New York: Houghton Mifflin.

Roger Tory Peterson. 2010. *Peterson Field Guide to Western Birds,* Fourth Edition. Boston: Houghton Mifflin Harcourt.

OTHER REGIONAL BIRDING RESOURCES

Fourteen local *Audubon Society* chapters exist throughout the Puget Sound Region. They provide an excellent means to learn more about birds. Most chapters have a newsletter, meetings, and local field trips to search for birds. Many have web sites with information about good places to go birding. Visit Audubon Washington at http://wa.audubon.org/audubon-locations and follow the chapter links.

BirdWeb (at www.birdweb.org), created by the Seattle Audubon Society, is an excellent resource for information on the birds of the Puget Sound Region.

Tweeters is an e-mail list on birds and birding sponsored by the Burke Museum at the University of Washington. Some 2,000 subscribers make Tweeters a lively forum and a good place to keep up with interesting bird sightings in the Region. Visit the Tweeters web site at www.scn.org/tweeters/ for subscription instructions.

The *Washington Ornithological Society* (WOS) – open to all persons interested in birds – offers monthly meetings in Seattle, field trips, a newsletter and other publications, and an annual conference. Visit the WOS web site at www.wos.org for information on membership and upcoming activities.

The Tweeters and Washington Ornithological Society web sites offer useful links to other birding resources.

NATURE STORES

Seattle Audubon Society Nature Shop, 8050 35th Avenue NE, Seattle, WA 98115 (phone 206-523-4483, www.seattleaudubon.org/sas/TheNatureShop.aspx) has a fine selection of books along with seed, bird feeders, and optics. A number of other local Audubon Society chapters also sell seed, bird feeders, and books.

There are a number of Wild Birds Unlimited stores in the region as well as other nature shops. Their staffs are always eager to answer your bird and bird-feeding questions. The yellow pages of the telephone directory will locate the closest nature store.

Species Accounts

The following pages present accounts and photographs of the most familiar bird species of the Puget Sound Region. Information on each species is presented in a standardized format: see the sample page (opposite) for an explanation. Species are grouped by families, color-coded and thumb-indexed. A dozen species found mostly in the mountains are presented separately at the end (pages 374–381). The Quick Guide on the first page inside the front cover of the book will help you locate the birds.

The following terms are used to describe the relative abundance of each species and the likelihood of finding it in a particular season. These definitions were developed by the American Birding Association.

- **Common:** Found in moderate to large numbers, and easily found in appropriate habitat at the right time of year.
- **Fairly Common:** Found in small to moderate numbers, and usually easy to find in appropriate habitat at the right time of year.
- **Uncommon:** Found in small numbers, and usually – but not always – found with some effort in appropriate habitat at the right time of year.
- **Rare:** Occurs annually in very small numbers. Not to be expected on any given day, but may be found with extended effort over the course of the appropriate season(s).

Birds shown in the photographs in the Species Accounts are adults unless the captions indicate otherwise.

NAME OF THE SPECIES
Its Latin name

Description: Length (and wingspan for larger species), followed by a description that includes differences in plumages between sexes and ages. Key field marks – unique markings visible in the field that help distinguish one species from another – are shown in **boldfaced** type.

Similar Species: Identifies similar-appearing species and describes how to tell them apart.

Seasonal Abundance: Identifies the times of year that the species is here and its relative abundance (see facing page for definitions of abundance terms). Also describes its overall range.

Where to Find: Explains generally where this bird may be found in the Puget Sound Region; may also suggest some of the better locations to search for it.

Habitat: Describes the habitat(s) in which this bird is normally found in the Puget Sound Region.

Diet and Behavior: Identifies the prime sources of food and highlights behaviors characteristic of this species.

Voice: Describes the main song and calls of the species.

Did you know? Provides interesting facts about this species.

Date & Location Seen: A place for you to record the date and location of your first sighting of this species.

Description: 28″, wingspan 54″. White goose with **black wingtips**, pinkish legs, **pink bill with blackish "grinning patch"**. JUVENILE: Dusky upperparts, grayish legs. Dark variant called Blue Goose (rare in Region) gray with white head, neck.

Similar Species: Swans larger without black wingtips. Ross's Goose (not shown; rare in Region) smaller with stubby bill.

Seasonal Abundance: Common but very local winter resident in Region, arrives October, departs by May. Breeds on Arctic tundra from northeastern Russia east to Greenland, winters to northern Mexico. Most birds wintering in Region come from Wrangel Island, Siberia.

Where to Find: Local wintering grounds mostly limited to Fir Island, Stillaguamish River delta near Stanwood. Stragglers or California-bound migrants occasionally noted elsewhere in lowlands.

Habitat: Short-grass or post-production agricultural fields, estuaries.

Diet and Behavior: Forages mostly on land but also in shallow water, almost entirely on plant materials including grasses, shoots, waste grain. Highly gregarious. Noisy, single-species flocks number in tens of thousands, appear blizzard-like when flushed by marauding eagle.

Voice: Highly vocal. Raucous, high-pitched, honking yelps.

Did you know? Snow Geese are often called "wavies" due to the undulating, irregular waves they form in flight.

Date & Location Seen: _____

Gray-bellied form

Description: 24", wingspan 42". Stocky, short-necked, **small-billed goose**, mostly blackish with black bill, legs; white rump, undertail; barred whitish flanks; **white neck-ring**. JUVENILE: Lacks neck-ring in fall.

Similar Species: Cackling Goose, Canada Goose (page 31) with white chin patch; most races larger, with longer bill.

Seasonal Abundance: Common but local winter resident in Region; arrives November, departs by May. Numbers swelled by spring migrants, February–March. Breeds on high-latitude tundra in North America, Eurasia; winters mostly to temperate zone.

Where to Find: Inland marine waters, rarely seen away from salt water. Good locations include Dungeness, Birch Bay, Padilla Bay, Alki Point in Seattle.

Habitat: Coastline, including bays, estuaries – often with gravel bottom.

Diet and Behavior: Forages by grazing on tidal flats, wading, upending in water. Diet almost exclusively leafy marine vegetation such as eelgrass. Highly gregarious. Rarely flocks with other species although may use same habitats. Flies low over ocean in ragged lines.

Voice: Quietly-murmured, nasal *rrok rrok*.

Did you know? The four recognized forms of this widely-distributed goose may be considered separate species in the future. Typical West Coast birds have dark bellies, while the West Atlantic subspecies is whiter below with a partial neck ring. Birds from an intermediate population wintering in Padilla Bay have gray bellies.

Date & Location Seen: _____

Canada Goose

Canada Goose (left), Cackling Goose (right)

Description: Variable. Smallest Cackling 22", wingspan 43"; largest Canada 43", wingspan 60". Both mostly grayish-brown with black legs, bill, tail; white rump, undertail; **black head, neck with white chin patch**.

Similar Species: Brant (page 29) lacks white chin patch. Greater White-fronted Goose (not shown; uncommon in Region) has yellow legs, lacks chin patch.

Seasonal Abundance: CACKLING: Uncommon migrant, winter resident in Region. CANADA: Common migrant, resident in Region. Migratory races of both arrive October, depart by May. Range throughout North America south to northern Mexico (Cackling mostly in West).

Where to Find: Throughout lowlands; less common to moderate elevations. Cackling usually with Canada flocks.

Habitat: Ponds, lakes, marshes, grassy fields, estuaries, rivers.

Diet and Behavior: Forage mostly on land but also in water, primarily for plant materials. Canada did not formerly breed in Region, but introduced populations have become habituated to humans, now thrive year round in urban areas.

Voice: Honk; smaller races of Cackling higher-pitched yelping.

Did you know? Three races of Cackling Goose and four of Canada Goose occur in the Puget Sound Region. Small, dark, short-necked races of Cackling are easily distinguished from large, light-breasted races of Canada, but intermediate races can be difficult to separate.

Date & Location Seen: _____

Trumpeter Swan

Tundra Swan

TRUMPETER SWAN / TUNDRA SWAN
Cygnus buccinator / Cygnus columbianus

Description: 60" / 52", wingspan 80" / 66". Huge, white, **long-necked** waterfowl with black bill as adults, juvenile bill pinkish. TRUMPETER: Larger; long **black bill extends to eye in broad triangle**; juvenile retains gray plumage throughout spring. TUNDRA: Smaller; **bill tapers to thin horizontal line at eye**; usually patch of yellow skin below eye; **juvenile white by spring**.

Similar Species: Snow Goose (page 27) smaller, has black wingtips. Introduced Mute Swan (not shown) has orange bill with black knob at base.

Seasonal Abundance: Common winter residents in Region (early November–March). TRUMPETER: Breeds south-central Alaska, other scattered locations in western North America. TUNDRA: Breeds on high tundra in Eurasia, North America, winters to temperate zone.

Where to Find: Lowlands, primarily northern portion of Region (Whatcom, Skagit, Snohomish Counties).

Habitat: Ponds, marshes, coastal bays, agricultural fields.

Diet and Behavior: Forage on plant materials on land or in water, including waste grains, potatoes. Gregarious, often in flocks including both species; may roost on open water.

Voice: TRUMPETER: Lower-pitched, like trumpet. TUNDRA: Gooselike barking *klow wow*.

Did you know? The Trumpeter Swan, close to extinction a century ago, is rapidly recovering. Birds wintering in Washington come from populations that nest in Alaska.

Date & Location Seen: _____

Male

Female

Description: 17", wingspan 30". Unique, short-necked duck with long, broad tail, **swept-back crest**, white belly, dark-blue speculum bordered at rear by white. MALE: Spectacularly **multicolored**. Green head; white partial neck collar, face pattern; scarlet eye-ring, bill base. Dull in summer, retaining head pattern, red bill. FEMALE: Brownish with broad **teardrop-shaped eye-ring**.

Similar Species: Mandarin Duck (not shown; introduced from Asia, rare in Region). Male gaudy with white face, orange "side-whiskers"; females closely similar but Mandarin with lighter head, upperparts; eye-ring smaller.

Seasonal Abundance: Fairly common summer resident in Region; uncommon, local in winter (beginning October); migrants return March. Ranges across U.S., southern Canada; winters to Mexico, Caribbean.

Where to Find: Lowlands to moderate elevations.

Habitat: Wooded swamps, ponds; shady, slow rivers; rarely open lakes.

Diet and Behavior: Forages mostly in water, seldom upending. Diet mainly seeds; takes more insects in summer. Nests in cavities. Almost as likely to be seen on tree branches as in water. Disperses late summer–fall, may gather in small groups outside nesting season.

Voice: Male gives thin, high whistles, female penetrating *ooo eeek* when flushed or alarmed.

Did you know? Threatened with extinction a century ago by over-hunting, Wood Ducks have recovered, aided in part by

Date & Location Seen: _____

Male

Female

Description: 19", wingspan 33". Medium-sized, rather plain dabbling duck with **white belly**, steep forehead, yellow feet, **white patch in speculum**. MALE: Mostly plain, variegated gray with back plumes, puffy head shape, dark bill, **black rump, undertail**; dull as female in summer. FEMALE: Mottled brown with yellowish-orange on sides of bill.

Similar Species: Female Mallard (page 41) longer, more bulky, lacks white speculum.

Seasonal Abundance: Common year-round resident in Region. Ranges across North America, Eurasia in middle latitudes, winters to subtropics.

Where to Find: Throughout lowlands, including urbanized corridor in southern part of Region.

Habitat: Ponds, lakes, marshes, estuaries. Prefers fresh water.

Diet and Behavior: Forages primarily for plant material, dabbling at surface, upending, or occasionally grazing on land. Sociable, often flocking with other dabblers. Pair formation begins by fall.

Voice: Male with unique, low-pitched *reb reb* call, also squeaky whistle. Female gives nasal quack.

Did you know? Gadwalls were historically present in much lower numbers in the Puget Sound Region. They increased dramatically due to removal of the coniferous forest in urban areas and to the spread of milfoil, an invasive water plant that is a favored food.

Date & Location Seen: _____

Eurasian Wigeon
Male

American Wigeon
Male

American Wigeon
Female

Eurasian Wigeon / American Wigeon
Anas penelope / Anas americana

Description: 19″, wingspan 32″. Short-necked dabbling ducks with **bluish-gray bill**, relatively long tail, **white forewing patch**. EURASIAN: **Gray sides**, white flanks, black undertail, **reddish head, yellowish forehead**. AMERICAN: Similar with **brownish sides, gray head, white forehead, green behind eye**. Females, summer males duller.

Similar Species: Gadwall (page 37) has white in speculum, not forewing; female has yellow on bill.

Seasonal Abundance: EURASIAN: Uncommon winter resident in Region, in flocks of Americans (arrives later). Ranges across Eurasia, winters to tropics; some stray to North America. AMERICAN: Common winter resident in Region, arrives late August, departs by May; very rare breeder. Breeds across North America, winters to Central America.

Where to Find: Widespread in lowlands. Eurasians usually easy to find at Samish Flats, Dungeness; often one or two in American Wigeon flocks at city parks, e.g., Green Lake (Seattle).

Habitat: Ponds, marshes, estuaries, bays, short-grass fields.

Diet and Behavior: Mostly plant material. Graze more than other ducks. Forage in water by skimming surface, rarely upending; also steal plants from American Coots, diving ducks. Form large, tight flocks, especially on land.

Voice: Distinctive *wee whe whir* whistled by male; female with growling quack.

Did you know? Wigeons are called Baldpates by hunters.

Date & Location Seen: _____

Male

Female

Description: 22″, wingspan 35″. Large, **heavy-bodied** dabbling duck with orange legs, **blue speculum** bordered front, rear with white. MALE: Grayish sides with darker back, chestnut breast, white neck-ring, yellow bill, **iridescent-green head**; in summer dull as female. FEMALE: Mottled brown with blotchy yellowish bill.

Similar Species: In female-type plumage, told from other dabbling ducks by larger size, speculum pattern.

Seasonal Abundance: Common resident in Region; numbers augmented in winter with migrants from north. Ranges around northern hemisphere from subarctic to subtropics.

Where to Find: Widespread in Region, less common in mountains.

Habitat: Any fresh- or saltwater body, also grain fields, city parks.

Diet and Behavior: Forages in water – upending, skimming near surface, even diving (rarely), mostly for plant but also for animal material. Grazes on land for waste grain, grass, insects. In parks becomes habituated to humans, takes handouts. Strong flyer. Gregarious, often flocking with other ducks. Pair formation, courtship begin in fall, nesting as early as late March.

Voice: Female makes familiar quacking. Male offers single whistles while courting, grating calls in aggression.

Did you know? Mallards are the origin of every variety of domestic duck except the Muscovy.

Date & Location Seen: _____

Blue-winged Teal
Male

Blue-winged Teal
Female

Cinnamon Teal
Male

Description: 15", wingspan 23". Small dabblers with **long, dark bill**, green speculum, **powder-blue forewing patch visible in flight**. BLUE-WINGED: Male brown with white flank patch, head gray with **bold white crescent behind bill**; dull as female in summer. Female mottled brown with diffuse pale facial area behind bill. CINNAMON: Male **chestnut-red** with red eye; dull as female in summer. Female mottled brown with plain face. Nearly impossible to distinguish juvenile Blue-winged from Cinnamon Teal, but latter averages longer bill, plainer face.

Similar Species: Green-winged Teal (page 49) smaller, shorter-billed, lacks blue forewing patch.

Seasonal Abundance: BLUE-WINGED: Uncommon breeder in Region; much more common as late May migrant. Ranges Alaska, Labrador south to Texas, winters south to Brazil. CINNAMON: Fairly common breeder, present in Region from April through September; very rare in winter. Breeds western North America, winters south to Patagonia.

Where to Find: Mostly lowlands; sewage ponds particularly favored.

Habitat: Prefer fresh water in open areas: ponds, marshes, flooded fields.

Diet and Behavior: Both forage for plant, animal matter in shallows, rarely upending. Blue-winged eats more insects. Fast, agile fliers, frequently found in small groups of mixed species of teals.

Voice: Females quack; males chatter, whistle.

Did you know? Closely related, Blue-winged and Cinnamon Teals hybridize rarely but regularly.

Date & Location Seen: _____

Male

Female

Description: 18", wingspan 29". Fairly small dabbling duck with **very large spoon-shaped bill**, green speculum, orange legs, **powder-blue forewing patch visible in flight**. MALE: White breast, **rust-brown belly, sides**; iridescent-green head, yellow eye, black bill. Dull as female in summer. FEMALE: Mottled brown with dark eye, orangish bill.

Similar Species: Bill size, shape distinctive.

Seasonal Abundance: Common winter, fairly common summer resident in Region; numbers augmented when migrants arrive in late summer. Ranges across northern temperate zone of Old, New Worlds, winters to tropics.

Where to Find: Widespread in lowlands, often abundant in sewage lagoons.

Habitat: Ponds, lakes, marshes, estuaries, bays, flooded fields.

Diet and Behavior: Feeds while swimming, often in flocks in tight, circling masses. Forages by sweeping bill from side to side to skim, filter at surface for plant, animal matter, seldom upending. May mix with other ducks, but tends to flock with its own species. Courting, pair formation begin late winter; male attains breeding plumage later than other dabblers.

Voice: Male gives low calls during courtship; female quacks hoarsely.

Did you know? Shovelers' filter-feeding is facilitated by lamellae – transverse ridges inside the edges of the upper and lower bill that act as sieves, trapping food particles.

Date & Location Seen: _____

Male

Female

NORTHERN PINTAIL
Anas acuta

Description: 20″ (male 26″ with tail), wingspan 33″. **Slender**, long-necked dabbling duck with long, thin bill, **green speculum** bordered with buff at front, white at rear. MALE: Grayish with brown head, long, needle-like tail, **white on breast extending in thin line up side of neck**; dull as female in summer. FEMALE: Mottled grayish-brown with short, pointed tail, **dark-gray bill**.

Similar Species: In female-type plumage, slender shape, dark bill separate pintail from other dabblers.

Seasonal Abundance: Common winter resident in Region, rare breeder. Highly migratory with transients arriving by August, departing by May. Breeds from Arctic to middle latitudes in North America, Eurasia; winters to tropics.

Where to Find: Lowlands; much less common near urbanized areas.

Habitat: Ponds, marshes, estuaries, shallow lakes, flooded fields.

Diet and Behavior: Mostly dabbles in shallow water but may walk on land, foraging. Diet mainly plant material including waste grain, also takes insects, aquatic organisms. Gathers in large or small groups, often with other ducks. Courting, pair formation begin in winter.

Voice: Fairly vocal, male with fluty *toop toop*, also high buzzy calls; female quacks.

Did you know? Northern Pintail is the most abundant duck in the Pacific flyway. The North American population has been estimated at six million.

Date & Location Seen: _____

Male

Female

Description: 13″, wingspan 23″. **Small** dabbling duck with **short, dark bill, green speculum**. MALE: Grayish with chestnut-and-green head, yellow undertail, **white vertical bar on side**; dull as female in summer. FEMALE: Mottled brown with dark line through eye.

Similar Species: Smaller, more compact, shorter-billed than other dabblers; female eye-line more pronounced.

Seasonal Abundance: Common winter resident in Region, rare breeder. Highly migratory with transients arriving by August, departing by May. Breeds from Arctic to middle latitudes in North America, Eurasia; winters to tropics.

Where to Find: Mostly lowlands, rarely in mountains.

Habitat: Ponds, marshes, estuaries, bays, shallow lakes, flooded fields.

Diet and Behavior: Forages by dabbling in shallow water or walking on wet mud, filtering water for plant materials, small aquatic organisms. Gathers in large or small groups, often with other ducks. Flocks fly swiftly in tight units, leaving water quickly, apparently with little effort. Courting, pair formation begin in winter.

Voice: Male highly vocal with ringing *peep*; female gives weak, nasal quack.

Did you know? The Eurasian race, called Common Teal and sometimes considered a separate species, is a rare winter visitor to the Puget Sound Region. It is recognized by the horizontal instead of vertical white bar on the side.

Date & Location Seen: _____

Redhead Male

Male

Female

Description: 21", wingspan 29". Sleek, elegant, long-necked diving duck with **sloping forehead, long, dark bill**, plain-grayish wings. MALE: Black at both ends with **whitish back, sides. Head, neck chestnut-reddish**; eye red. FEMALE: Browner overall, lacks red head, eye.

Similar Species: Distinctive head shape, plumage separate Canvasback from scaups (page 55). Male **Redhead** (see inset; rare in Region) distinguished by **shape, pattern of head, bill, grayer back**.

Seasonal Abundance: Fairly common but local winter resident, arrives by October, most depart by April. Breeds in western North America from central Alaska to South Dakota, winters east to New England, south to Mexico.

Where to Find: Throughout lowlands. Good locations include Everett sewage ponds, Nisqually National Wildlife Refuge.

Habitat: Lakes, estuaries, coastal bays, sewage ponds, marshes with open water.

Diet and Behavior: Dives, mostly in shallow water, primarily for plant materials; may also dabble, take aquatic insects. Sociable; gathers in flocks, often with other ducks. Courts less on wintering grounds than other ducks, as most pair formation occurs later in spring on migration.

Voice: Female grunts, male cooing sounds seldom heard in Region.

Did you know? The Canvasback's Latin species name, *valisineria*, refers to wild celery – an important food item.

Date & Location Seen: _____

Male

Female

Description: 17", wingspan 24". Short-necked diving duck with **peaked head, pale ring near tip of gray bill**, grayish wings in flight. MALE: Purplish-iridescent head, **black back**, breast; **vertical white mark on gray side** in front of wing. FEMALE: Brownish with **white eye-ring**, diffuse pale facial area near bill.

Similar Species: Lesser Scaup (page 55) head less peaked, no ring on bill, male with gray back, female with bold white face patch at bill base.

Seasonal Abundance: Common winter resident in Region, arrives by September, most depart by May; rare summer resident. Nests northern North America from western Alaska to Labrador, winters to Central America, Caribbean.

Where to Find: Mostly lowlands, where widespread; has nested in San Juan, Thurston Counties.

Habitat: Ponds, lakes, sewage lagoons, marshes, coastal bays, rivers. Prefers fresh water.

Diet and Behavior: Mostly dives, but may also dabble in fairly shallow water. Diet aquatic plants, insects. Sociable. Flocks may be large or small, single-species or mixed with other divers on large water bodies; also flocks with dabblers on small ponds.

Voice: Male whistles, female growls softly.

Did you know? Unlike other diving ducks, Ring-necked Ducks are able to spring directly off the water into flight, enabling them to use small ponds surrounded by trees.

Date & Location Seen: _____

Greater Scaup
Female

Greater Scaup
Male

Lesser Scaup
Male

Description: 18″ / 17″, wingspan 28″ / 26″. Short-necked diving ducks with bluish-gray bills, **white wing stripes** visible in flight. MALES: **Blackish on both ends, whitish in middle**, head darkly iridescent. FEMALES: Brownish with **white facial patch at bill base**. GREATER: **Head round**, neck thicker, bill wider, male's head glosses greenish. LESSER: **Peaked crown**, neck thinner, bill smaller, **wing stripe extends only halfway to wingtip**, male's head glosses purplish.

Similar Species: Ring-necked Duck (page 53) head more peaked, ring near bill tip; male with black back, vertical white mark on side.

Seasonal Abundance: Common winter residents in Region. GREATER: Arrives by October, departs in May. Breeds around world in far north, winters to temperate zone. LESSER: Arrives by October, most depart by April; rare breeder at marshy sewage ponds. Breeds western North America (Alaska to Colorado); winters south as far as Colombia.

Where to Find: Mostly lowlands.

Habitat: Lakes, sewage lagoons, coastal bays, estuaries, rivers. GREATER: Prefers saltwater habitats but not exclusively.

Diet and Behavior: Dive for mollusks, other aquatic animals, plants. Highly gregarious, gathering in tight flocks, often including both scaup species, other ducks.

Voice: Grating sounds, deep whistles.

Did you know? Hunters refer to both species of scaups as Bluebills.

Date & Location Seen: _____

Male

Female

Description: 16", wingspan 26". Compact, round-headed diving duck with **steep forehead, stubby bill**. MALE: Darkly-colored, mostly **slate-blue with rusty sides, bold white marks** on head, sides, back; dull as female in summer. FEMALE: Brown with white belly, white spot on cheek, another near bill base.

Similar Species: Female scoters (pages 59–63) much heavier with larger bills, sloping foreheads; female Bufflehead (page 67) smaller with white wing patch, only one face patch.

Seasonal Abundance: Fairly common coastal resident in Region, less so in spring when breeding in mountains where uncommon. Breeds in eastern, western North America, Iceland, eastern Asia; winters coastally to temperate zone.

Where to Find: Coastline; less common in southern part of Region. Cascades, Olympics in spring, summer. Good locations include Ediz Hook, Alki Beach (West Seattle). Breeders rarely observed, but Skykomish, Dungeness Rivers worth checking.

Habitat: Rocky coastline including bays, exposed locations; breeds on mountain streams.

Diet and Behavior: Forages mostly by diving for mollusks, marine organisms, insects; may also dabble at surface. Gregarious. Courtship begins in winter, pairs form in spring, move up rivers to nest.

Voice: Male has piercing whistle, female nasal quacks.

Did you know? Female Harlequin Ducks may share in the care of mixed broods.

Date & Location Seen: _____

Male

Female

Description: 20", wingspan 30". **Stocky** diving duck with broad, **bulging bill, sloping forehead**, white eye. MALE: All-black with fleshy **orange-yellow-white bill, white patches on forehead, back of neck**, side of bill. FEMALE: Brownish-gray with whitish patches near bill base, on cheek. JUVENILE: Duller than adult, with pale belly, dark eye.

Similar Species: Black Scoter (page 63) female has entire lower face whitish, male without white on head, although immature Surf Scoter may also lack this. White-winged Scoter (page 61) has white speculum. Bill shape distinguishes from other ducks in Region.

Seasonal Abundance: Common winter resident in Region, most arrive by August, depart in May. A few non-breeders in summer. Nests in far north of continent (western Alaska to Labrador), winters coastally to Baja California, Georgia.

Where to Find: Widespread.

Habitat: Coastal bays, estuaries, exposed surf, rarely fresh water (in migration).

Diet and Behavior: Forages by diving, almost exclusively for mollusks while in winter quarters, also other aquatic organisms, plant material. Dives by jumping forward with partially-opened wings. Gregarious, often flocking with other scoter species. Pairs form during winter, spring.

Voice: Male whistles, female utters croaking grunts.

Did you know? In heavy surf, Surf Scoters synchronize their dives with breaking waves, diving just before the crash.

Date & Location Seen: _____

Female

Male

Description: 22", wingspan 33". **Large** diving duck, **white speculum** visible while flying, diving but may be obscured when at rest. MALE: All-black with white eye, small **white mark behind eye, reddish bill** with small black knob at base. FEMALE: Brownish-gray with dark eye, whitish facial patches. JUVENILE: Duller than adult, with pale belly.

Similar Species: Other scoters (pages 59, 63) smaller, lack white speculum; Surf Scoter has different bill shape. Pigeon Guillemot (page 187) smaller with weak flight, white patch at front of wing.

Seasonal Abundance: Common winter resident in Region (decreasing in recent years), most arrive by October, depart in May. A few non-breeders in summer. Nests in Alaska, western Canada, Eurasia, winters to temperate zone.

Where to Find: Less abundant than Surf Scoter but still rather common, widespread.

Habitat: Coastal bays, estuaries, rarely fresh water (mostly in migration).

Diet and Behavior: Dives with partially-opened wings for mollusks, small fish, other marine organisms, plant material. Gregarious, often flocking with other scoters; pairs form on winter quarters. Appears heavy in flight. Flocks move in long, wavering lines low over water.

Voice: Male whistles; female grunts seldom heard.

Did you know? The Eurasian race of the species is called Velvet Scoter.

Date & Location Seen: _____

Male

Female

Description: 19", wingspan 28". **Stocky** diving duck with **fairly small black bill**. MALE: All-black with fleshy **yellowish-orange knob** at bill base. FEMALE: Brownish-gray with **entire lower face, cheek whitish-gray**. JUVENILE: Similar to female, with pale belly.

Similar Species: Bill much smaller, held more horizontal than other scoters (pages 59–61). Female smaller with more extensive cheek patch (other female scoters have two smaller, whitish face patches). White-winged has white speculum. Ruddy Duck (page 77) smaller with large, broad bill, longer tail.

Seasonal Abundance: Mostly uncommon (locally fairly common) winter resident in Region, arrives by November, departs by April. Breeds on tundra, winters in temperate zone, of North America, East Asia. Formerly treated as single species with Common Scoter of Old World.

Where to Find: Inland marine waters. Good bets include Alki Point in Seattle, Drayton Harbor, Dungeness National Wildlife Refuge.

Habitat: Coastal waters with rocky bottoms.

Diet and Behavior: Primarily mollusks obtained by diving; also takes other marine organisms, insects, plant material. Gregarious, flocking with other scoters often in fairly tight groups. Courtship progresses throughout winter to spring.

Voice: More vocal than other scoters: grunts, whistles.

Did you know? Black is the least common scoter in the Region. Some 250,000 breed in Alaska, yet fewer than 5,000 winter on the Pacific Coast south of Anchorage.

Date & Location Seen: _____

Male Non-breeding

Female Non-breeding

Description: 16″ (male 21″ with tail), wingspan 28″. Short-necked, white-bellied, **stubby-billed** diving duck, short **blackish wings**. Plumage unusually variable due to three annual adult molts. MALE: Elegant, usually with **long, pointed tail;** bill dark with pink band. Breeding (spring) plumage mostly black with white face, non-breeding (winter) **mostly white** with black back, breast, neck patch. FEMALE: Bill bluish-green; dark overall, face whitish in non-breeding plumage.

Similar Species: In flight, combination of dark wings, whitish body unique among ducks. Markings different from Northern Pintail (page 47), neck longer than alcids (pages 185–191).

Seasonal Abundance: Fairly common but local winter resident in Region, arrives mid-October, departs by May. Breeds on Arctic tundra in Old, New Worlds, winters to temperate zone.

Where to Find: Inland marine waters. Rare in southern part of Region; look for it especially in north (e.g., Drayton Harbor), west (e.g., Sequim Bay).

Habitat: Coastal waters, extremely rarely on fresh water in Region.

Diet and Behavior: Dives for mollusks, other marine organisms, some plant material. Sociable, although flocks in Region smaller than in most of range.

Voice: Male very vocal with loud yodeling when spring courtship begins in winter quarters. Female gives soft grunts.

Did you know? Accomplished divers, Long-tailed Ducks have been recorded at depths exceeding 200 feet.

Date & Location Seen: _____

Male

Female

Description: 13″, wingspan 20″. **Small**, plump diving duck, with **small gray bill**, white belly, white wing patches easily visible in flight. MALE: Mostly white with dark back, iridescent-blackish, **puffy head with white patch at back**. FEMALE: Dull-grayish with **small, oval white cheek patch**, smaller wing patches than male.

Similar Species: Goldeneyes (page 69) larger, white patch of male below rather than behind eye. Hooded Merganser (page 71) male has rusty sides with black-and-white bars. Ruddy Duck (page 77) has larger bill, cheek patch.

Seasonal Abundance: Common winter resident in Region. Most arrive October, depart by May; rare in summer. Nests in interior from central Alaska to Québec, winters on both coasts from Aleutians, Maritimes south to Mexico.

Where to Find: Throughout lowlands.

Habitat: Adaptable. Found on fresh-, saltwater bodies of all sizes, even flooded fields.

Diet and Behavior: Dives for insects, other aquatic organisms, plant materials. Usually in small groups, but large concentrations occur at favorable sites. Patters on surface with rapid wing-beats before flying.

Voice: Fairly quiet in winter quarters but soft, growling whistles, grunts occasionally given.

Did you know? *Bucephala* – the scientific name of the genus – comes from a Greek word meaning ox-headed. The species' English name evokes the high, domed forehead of the American bison (buffalo).

Date & Location Seen: _____

Common Goldeneye Male

Common Goldeneye Female

Barrow's Goldeneye Male

Barrow's Goldeneye Female

Common Goldeneye / Barrow's Goldeneye
Bucephala clangula / Bucephala islandica

Description: 18", wingspan 27". Plump, short-necked, with short bill, **puffy head, white wing patch**. MALES: White with black-and-white back, dark iridescent head, white patch below eye. FEMALES: Grayish with brown head. COMMON: Head peaked in middle, male's **green with round patch**; less black on back. BARROW'S: Head peaked at front, **steep forehead**, bill smaller. Male's **head purplish, patch crescent-shaped**; less white on back.

Similar Species: Bufflehead (page 67) smaller, male's head patch behind rather than below eye.

Seasonal Abundance: Fairly common winter residents in Region. COMMON: Arrives by November, departs by April, rarely present in summer. Breeds across northern North America, Eurasia, winters to temperate zone. BARROW'S: Arrives in lowlands by October, departs by April; uncommon breeder in Cascades. Breeds Alaska south to Wyoming, Oregon, also northeastern Canada, Iceland; winters down both coasts in temperate zone.

Where to Find: Lowlands. BARROW'S: Summer in mountains.

Habitat: COMMON: Coastal bays, rivers, lakes, sewage ponds. BARROW'S: Mostly marine waters, often near dock pilings; nests on forested lakes.

Diet and Behavior: Dive for aquatic animals, plants; form loose flocks outside nesting season. Nest in tree cavities; courting, displaying already by fall arrival.

Voice: Soft grunts.

Did you know? Goldeneyes' wings create a loud whistling sound in flight.

Date & Location Seen: ───────────────

Male

Female

Description: 16", wingspan 23". Small, **long-tailed** duck with thin, **saw-toothed bill**, conspicuous **puffy crest**, white belly. Small white wing patches visible in flight. MALE: Striking; mostly blackish above including bill, with fan-shaped white crest, rusty sides, black-and-white side bars, ornamental back plumes; dull as female in late summer. FEMALE: Brownish-gray with yellowish-edged bill.

Similar Species: Other mergansers (pages 73–75) larger, with reddish bills. Bufflehead (page 67) female smaller with small cheek patch; male has white sides.

Seasonal Abundance: Fairly common resident in Region, less common in summer. Ranges across North America from southeastern Alaska, Washington, to Great Lakes, New Brunswick; winters to California, southeastern states.

Where to Find: Mostly lowlands, rarely to higher elevations.

Habitat: Breeds at wooded freshwater ponds, sloughs, sluggish creeks with emergent vegetation. Migrants, wintering groups also use estuaries, sewage ponds.

Diet and Behavior: Forages visually by diving, swimming underwater for fish, aquatic insects, other organisms. Usually in small groups, but may concentrate at favorable sites in fall. Often allows close approach, then patters along surface with rapid wing-beats, flies off. Nests in tree cavities, also nest boxes.

Voice: Fairly vocal with soft croaks.

Did you know? Hooded Mergansers occasionally hybridize with other cavity-nesting ducks, especially goldeneyes.

Date & Location Seen: _____

Male

Female

Description: 24", wingspan 34". **Robust**, white-bellied diving duck, with thin, **reddish saw-toothed bill, shaggy crest**. Large white wing patches visible in flight. MALE: Body mostly white with dark-green head, dark back; dull as female in late summer. FEMALE: Gray with brown head, white chin.

Similar Species: Red-breasted Merganser (page 75) female very similar but less bulky, with neither distinct white throat nor abrupt line between light-gray body, brown head; bill thinner at base. Hooded Merganser (page 71) much smaller, bill not reddish.

Seasonal Abundance: Common resident in Region. Ranges across forested areas of northern hemisphere to southern edge of temperate zone.

Where to Find: Throughout Region, sea level to mountain passes.

Habitat: Prefers forested areas with fresh, clear water (rivers, lakes), but also coastal bays; often in brackish river mouths.

Diet and Behavior: Forages visually by diving, swimming underwater, mostly for fish; young eat aquatic insects. Concentrates in large flocks from late summer to early winter in rivers, coastal estuaries where pair formation begins. Nests near water in tree cavities, mostly along major rivers, but also near clear lakes; may be loosely colonial.

Voice: Hoarse croaking notes.

Did you know? In the Old World this species is called Goosander.

Date & Location Seen: _____

Male

Female

Description: 22", wingspan 30". **Slim**, long-necked, white-bellied diving duck with long, thin, **reddish saw-toothed bill**, conspicuous **shaggy crest**. Large **white wing patches** visible in flight. MALE: Elegant with green head, white neck-ring, dark back, gray sides; dull as female in late summer. FEMALE: Gray with brown head.

Similar Species: Common Merganser (page 73) female very similar but bulkier, with distinct white throat, abrupt line between light-gray body, brown head; bill thicker at base. Hooded Merganser (page 71) smaller, bill not reddish.

Seasonal Abundance: Common winter resident in Region, rare in summer. Most arrive October, depart by April. Breeds across northern North America, Eurasia to tree line, winters coastally to subtropics.

Where to Find: Widespread throughout Region on sheltered marine waters.

Habitat: Coastal bays, estuaries; extremely rare on fresh water in Region.

Diet and Behavior: Forages by diving, swimming underwater, mostly for fish. Loose flocks occasionally fish cooperatively by herding schooling fish. Courtship behavior increases throughout late fall, winter as males attain breeding plumage.

Voice: Relatively silent. Females may give harsh, grating squawks.

Did you know? One of the fastest-flying ducks, Red-breasted Mergansers have been clocked at 100 miles per hour.

Date & Location Seen: _____

Male Breeding

Female

Description: 15", wingspan 19". Compact, **large-headed, broad-billed** diving duck with **long, stiff tail** often cocked upward. MALE: In breeding plumage (spring–summer) reddish-brown with black head, neck, **white cheek, powder-blue bill**; dull-brown in fall–winter (retains black cap, white cheek). FEMALE: Brownish, **light cheek crossed by dark line**.

Similar Species: Fairly unique. Female Bufflehead (page 67) has smaller bill, cheek patch.

Seasonal Abundance: Locally common winter resident in Region, uncommon breeder. Nests western North America; winters in southern U.S, along both coasts, south through Mexico. Also resident western South America.

Where to Find: Lowlands: fresh water, protected coastal sites.

Habitat: Ponds, lakes, sewage lagoons, bays. Breeds on fresh water with marshy edge.

Diet and Behavior: Dives, feeds mostly on aquatic plants, some insects. Sits low in water when active but sleeps buoyantly on surface. Often in large groups when not nesting. Patters along water, flapping short wings rapidly to take flight; clumsy on land. Male courtship unique – raises tail to expose white under it, pumps head rapidly, followed by boisterous rushes across water.

Voice: Courting male produces stuttering series of ticks while pumping bill against inflated throat; female gives nasal call in defense of young.

Did you know? Unlike other ducks, Ruddies molt to dull plumage in fall and winter.

Date & Location Seen: _____

Male

Female

Description: 10", wingspan 14". Elegantly-plumaged little gamefowl with **forward-drooping topknot. Grayish overall, scaled belly**, brown sides with lighter barring. MALE: Chestnut patch on belly, **white eyebrow, black throat outlined in white**.

Similar Species: Two other quails rare in Region (not shown). Mountain Quail has long, upright head plume, plain belly, chestnut throat. Northern Bobwhite browner, with patterned back, unscaled belly, pale throat, no topknot.

Seasonal Abundance: Fairly common resident in Region. Somewhat cyclical; high brood mortality in wet years. Native along Pacific Coast from southern Oregon through Baja California; introduced north to Washington, southern British Columbia.

Where to Find: Lowlands. Most numerous in driest parts of Region – Sequim-Dungeness, Whidbey Island, San Juans, South Sound Prairies.

Habitat: Dry-climate species; around Puget Sound, gets by in prairie landscapes or where forests removed or fragmented. Needs shrub cover next to open ground for foraging.

Diet and Behavior: Eats mostly plant material (seeds, leaves, etc.), some invertebrates. Sociable. Coveys disband for breeding but stay within winter territory. Prolific – two broods some years, up to 20 eggs per clutch.

Voice: Loud *chi ca go* assembly call; variety of other contact, alarm, advertising calls.

Did you know? Coveys post sentries to warn of danger. Look for them on fenceposts or other prominent perches.

Date & Location Seen: _____

Male

Female

RING-NECKED PHEASANT
Phasianus colchicus

Description: 21" (male 30" with tail), wingspan 31". Large, **chicken-like** bird with **long tail**. Mostly mottled shades of brown. MALE: More colorful – orangish flanks, gray rump, **white neck-ring, iridescent-green head, red skin on face**.

Similar Species: Other large "chickens" in Region shorter-tailed, males drab; usually found in forests. Ruffed Grouse (page 83) smaller; Sooty Grouse (page 375) gray.

Seasonal Abundance: Uncommon year-round resident in Region. Native to Asia, widely introduced as game bird elsewhere.

Where to Find: Rural, semi-rural lowlands, e.g., Kitsap Peninsula, Vashon Island, Sequim-Dungeness, Kent Valley, Seattle's Discovery Park. Pen-raised birds released for hunting help sustain naturalized populations.

Habitat: Open fields, brush patches, woodland edges, lightly-developed residential areas, large parks.

Diet and Behavior: Forages on ground, also in brush, trees. Opportunistic. Consumes agricultural grains, weed seeds, roots, fruits, nuts, leaves, insects (adults, larvae), earthworms, snails. Prefers to walk or run but strong flyer when flushed. Takes off explosively on whirring wings. Young follow female, forage for themselves upon hatching. May form flocks in winter.

Voice: Male crowing, alarm call loud, grating *krrok ook*; also softer clucking sounds (both sexes).

Did you know? The first successful introduction of pheasants to the United States was in Oregon's Willamette Valley in 1882, followed by Washington in 1883.

Date & Location Seen: _____

Description: 18", wingspan 22". Variably brownish, cryptically patterned, **chicken-like** bird with barred flanks, small crest (sometimes flattened). Reddish to grayish **tail with black band near tip**.

Similar Species: Ring-necked Pheasant (page 81) much larger, long-tailed; usually found in open country. Sooty Grouse (page 375) somewhat larger, tail dark with gray tip, male uniformly darker; inhabits conifer forests.

Seasonal Abundance: Fairly common year-round resident in Region. Ranges across continent's northern forest zones.

Where to Find: Widespread along base of Cascades, Olympics, but secretive; usually detected by male's drumming or when female wanders into view with brood. Skagit River valley, Mount Rainier National Park, Black Hills near Olympia good bets.

Habitat: Low to mid-elevation deciduous or mixed forests with developed understory, ground layer, often along stream corridors.

Diet and Behavior: Leaves, fruits, other plant materials; buds important in winter. Chicks feed themselves upon hatching, mostly small invertebrates at first – can fly within week. Solitary in breeding season, may form small, loose winter flocks. Males "drum" from log, other ground perches, mostly in spring.

Voice: Unremarkable. Female sometimes makes clucking, cooing sounds.

Did you know? Drumming is an accelerating series of sonic booms as air rushes to fill the vacuum produced by the male's wing movements. Young birds require long practice to master the technique.

Date & Location Seen: _____

Non-breeding

Breeding

Description: 25", wingspan 36". Smallest loon. **Thin bill** appears slightly upcurved, **usually held slightly upward**. NON-BREEDING: **Pale** with white on face, throat, neck; **gray back speckled with white**. BREEDING: **Dark back**, gray head, neck, **red throat**.

Similar Species: Common Loon (page 89) larger with thicker bill, less white on face, neck in non-breeding plumage. Pacific Loon (page 87) about same size with straight bill usually held level.

Seasonal Abundance: Fairly common winter resident in Region, arrives September, departs by May. Breeds in Canada, Alaska, Eurasia, winters along coasts in temperate zone.

Where to Find: More prevalent in northern part of Region. Good places to check include Blaine, Fort Flagler State Park, Penn Cove, west shoreline of Whidbey Island from Point Partridge (Libbey Beach County Park) to Deception Pass.

Habitat: Shallow, protected saltwater bays, river mouths, rarely freshwater lakes.

Diet and Behavior: Mainly small fish obtained by diving. Usually feeds singly or in small flocks, sometimes in large flocks at prey concentrations.

Voice: In winter, usually silent.

Did you know? Red-throated Loon is the only loon that can take flight from land rather than running across the water.

Date & Location Seen: _____

Non-breeding

Breeding

Description: 26", wingspan 36". Smooth, **rounded head; slender bill** held horizontally. NON-BREEDING: **Dark back**, dark around eye, clean white throat, breast. **Dark back of neck sharply separated from white front of neck; thin, dark chin strap often visible**. BREEDING: **Pale-gray crown, nape**, black back with white checkering. **Dark throat patch, vertical white stripes on sides of neck**.

Similar Species: Red-throated Loon (page 85) holds bill slightly upward; more white on neck, face. Common Loon (page 89) larger with thicker bill, steep forehead; in non-breeding plumage, lacks clean separation between throat, back of neck; has white around eye.

Seasonal Abundance: Fairly common resident in Region, September–May. Breeds on Arctic tundra in Canada, Alaska, northeastern Siberia, winters farther south along coast on both sides of Pacific.

Where to Find: More common in northern part of Region – for example, around Bellingham, Drayton Harbor, San Juan Islands, Point Wilson, Marrowstone Point; also Cherry Point during April–May herring spawning season.

Habitat: Open salt water; prefers deeper waters than other loons.

Diet and Behavior: Small fish. Often seen in large, concentrated flocks where food supply abundant.

Voice: Calls mainly on breeding grounds.

Did you know? Pacific Loons migrate in flocks, more so than other loons.

Date & Location Seen: _____

Non-breeding

Breeding

Description: 32", wingspan 46". **Large** loon with **thick bill**, steep forehead. NON-BREEDING: White throat, **pale around eye**; back dark with lighter mottling. **Traces of white collar extending back on upper neck, dark collar extending forward on lower neck.** BREEDING: **Head, bill black; black collar, dark back checkered white.**

Similar Species: Yellow-billed Loon (not shown; rare in Region) similar but slightly larger with yellowish bill (Common's has dark ridge on top in non-breeding plumage). Red-throated Loon (page 85) more finely built; thin bill held slightly upward. Pacific Loon (page 87) smaller; in non-breeding plumage, sharp contrast between white throat, dark back of neck.

Seasonal Abundance: Common winter resident in Region; a few nest on isolated lakes, reservoirs in King, Whatcom Counties. Breeds across northern North America to Iceland, winters south along coasts.

Where to Find: In winter, anywhere on salt water (a few non-breeders also in summer). Common on Hood Canal, Saratoga Passage (east side of Whidbey Island).

Habitat: Winters on open salt water (occasionally freshwater lakes).

Diet and Behavior: Small fish caught, swallowed underwater. Usually forages singly.

Voice: Distinctive loud yodeling, mostly during breeding season but also sometimes in flight during migration.

Did you know? Nesting Common Loons require pristine conditions and are sensitive to human disturbance.

Date & Location Seen: _____

Breeding

Non-breeding

Description: 13", wingspan 16". **Brownish, short-necked, stocky** grebe with **thick, short, pale bill, white undertail**. BREEDING: Forehead, throat black, bill with black ring. Chicks show extensive head streaking.

Similar Species: Horned Grebe (page 93) has longer, thinner bill; head, neck contrasting black-and-white in non-breeding plumage. Red-necked Grebe (page 95) larger, longer-billed.

Seasonal Abundance: Fairly common breeder in Region, becomes common in winter as northern birds arrive. Ranges from Great Plains south to Central, South America, vacating cold interior in winter.

Where to Find: Throughout lowlands; also on higher-elevation lakes in migration. Nests in city parks with emergent vegetation, for example, Green Lake (Seattle), Union Bay Marsh (Seattle), Juanita Bay (Kirkland).

Habitat: Freshwater marshes, lakes, ponds, with smaller numbers on protected salt water in winter.

Diet and Behavior: Small fish, aquatic insects, crustaceans taken underwater. To submerge, may dive headfirst or simply allow itself to sink; often resurfaces some distance away. Rarely seen in flocks.

Voice: In breeding season, loud *cuck cuck cuck, cow cow cow, cowah cowah*.

Did you know? Pied-billed Grebe is the most widespread grebe in North America and in the Region.

Date & Location Seen: _____

Eared Grebe
Non-breeding

Non-breeding

Breeding

Description: 14″, wingspan 18″. Relatively flat head, red eye, straight bill with light tip. Rides low in water. NON-BREEDING: Back, back of neck, crown dark-gray; **front of neck, throat, cheeks whitish**. BREEDING: Back grayish, **neck reddish, head black with golden "ears" from eye to back of head**.

Similar Species: Eared Grebe (see inset; uncommon in Region in migration, winter) slighter, **bill thinner**; thin-necked, rides high in water. In non-breeding plumage, **cheek dark, top of head peaks above eye**. Neck blackish in breeding plumage. Pied-billed Grebe (page 91) overall brownish with thick bill. Western Grebe (page 97) larger with longer neck, bill.

Seasonal Abundance: Common winter resident in Region, late August–April. Breeds on interior lakes, marshes of northern North America, Eurasia; winters southward.

Where to Find: Widespread in lowlands.

Habitat: Saltwater bays, inlets, channels; smaller numbers on large freshwater lakes, slow-moving rivers.

Diet and Behavior: In winter, feeds mostly on small fish obtained by diving.

Voice: Mostly silent in winter; high, thin notes occasionally heard.

Did you know? Horned Grebes can stay submerged up to three minutes and swim 500 feet below the surface on one dive.

Date & Location Seen: _____

Non-breeding

Breeding

Description: 20", wingspan 24". Large, gray-brown grebe with dark eye, **flat, wedge-shaped head, thick neck, tapered yellowish bill**. NON-BREEDING: Back, crown dark; **cheek, neck dingy-gray, light ear patch**. BREEDING: **Black crown, reddish-brown neck, pale-gray cheeks, throat**.

Similar Species: More than twice as heavy as Horned Grebe (page 93), Pied-billed Grebe (page 91). Horned has shorter neck, thinner bill, red eye. Pied-billed brown overall with thick, stubby bill. Larger Western Grebe (page 97) clean gray-and-white with longer, thinner neck, bill.

Seasonal Abundance: Common winter resident throughout Region; begins returning late July, most depart March. Breeding range northern North America, Eurasia; winters south along coasts.

Where to Find: Widespread. Numerous at mouth of Hood Canal (Foulweather Bluff) in fall migration. Other typical sites Drayton Harbor, Cattle Point (San Juan Island), Deception Pass State Park. Lake Sammamish, Lake Washington, American Lake (Tacoma) good freshwater sites.

Habitat: Favors deep saltwater sites – open waters, large bays, inlets; much lower numbers on large lowland lakes.

Diet and Behavior: Dives for small fish.

Voice: Not often heard in winter.

Did you know? Red-necked Grebes nest on lakes in northeastern Washington. Like other grebes, they build floating nests and carry their young on their backs.

Date & Location Seen: _____

Description: 25", wingspan 24". **Long-necked, black-and-white** grebe with **long, thin dull-yellow bill**. Neck white in front, black behind. White throat, cheeks; black cap extends down to include red eye.

Similar Species: Clark's Grebe (not shown; rare winter visitor in Region) almost identical but lighter-appearing; bill orange-yellow, dark cap may not cover eye. Red-necked Grebe (page 95) has shorter neck, dark eye; in non-breeding plumage, neck gray (not white). Horned Grebe (page 93) smaller with short neck, smaller dark bill.

Seasonal Abundance: Common resident in Region, September–May; a few non-breeders present in summer. Nests on lakes in interior western North America (Manitoba to California); winters along coast from southeastern Alaska to northwestern Mexico.

Where to Find: Throughout Region. Good numbers usually at Quartermaster Harbor (Vashon–Maury Islands), Drayton Harbor, Hood Canal, Penn Cove, Saratoga Passage (Whidbey–Camano Islands), Elliott Bay, Lake Washington.

Habitat: Sheltered saltwater bays, inlets; also large freshwater lakes.

Diet and Behavior: Mostly fish, obtained by diving. Often forms large flocks in winter.

Voice: Loud, high, two-note *crick creek* call, given all year.

Did you know? Wintering populations of Western Grebe are declining in the Region.

Date & Location Seen: _____

Non-breeding

Description: 35", wingspan 48". **All-dark with buffy chin.** In flight, holds thick neck nearly straight, shows **short tail**. BREEDING: **Blue throat pouch** (visible at close range), fine white feathers on head, neck, back. IMMATURE: Plain dark-brown with tan breast.

Similar Species: Pelagic Cormorant (page 103) has thinner neck, head, bill; longer tail; white flank patch during breeding season. Double-crested Cormorant (page 101) has orange at lower base of bill; longer wings, tail; flies with noticeable crook in neck.

Seasonal Abundance: Fairly common for most of year in northern part of Region, less common in southern part; scarce or absent in nesting season. Breeds colonially along coast from southwestern British Columbia to Baja California.

Where to Find: Whidbey Island (west side), Marrowstone Point, Point Wilson, San Juan Islands ferry, among many other sites.

Habitat: Exclusively saltwater; rarely even flies over land.

Diet and Behavior: Dives for fish, crabs, shrimp. Gregarious. Flies in long lines low over water.

Voice: Usually silent except at nest.

Did you know? Brandt's Cormorants nest on rocky islands and headlands on Washington's outer coast. Like other cormorants they feed their young through regurgitation of partially digested fish.

Date & Location Seen: _____

Non-breeding

Immature

DOUBLE-CRESTED CORMORANT
Phalacrocorax auritus

Description: 32", wingspan 52". **All-dark** with long tail, thick neck, **orange facial skin, throat pouch**. In flight, **holds thick neck with pronounced crook**. BREEDING: **White tufts behind eye**. IMMATURE: Brown with paler breast, neck.

Similar Species: Brandt's (page 99), Pelagic (page 103) Cormorants have shorter wings, fly with neck held straighter. Pelagic's bill, head, neck much thinner. In breeding plumage, Pelagic has white flank patch, red skin on face. Brandt's has buffy chin in all plumages.

Seasonal Abundance: Common resident in Region; numbers increase in winter. Nests along both coasts of North America, also interior of continent. Winters along coasts south to Gulf of California, Gulf of Mexico.

Where to Find: Throughout lowlands. Often perches on pilings, logs, docks, sandbars, rocks. Large breeding colonies at Port Gardner Bay, Everett.

Habitat: Saltwater bays, estuaries, shorelines; freshwater lakes, ponds, rivers, marshes. Only local cormorant likely on fresh water.

Diet and Behavior: Dives for small fish. Sometimes flies high in V formation like geese. Swims low in water with head tilted slightly upward. Often perches with wings outstretched to dry them.

Voice: Quiet away from breeding grounds.

Did you know? Double-crested Cormorant is the most widespread cormorant in North America. Its population in the Puget Sound Region is increasing.

Date & Location Seen: _____

Breeding

Description: 27", wingspan 39". **Smallest local cormorant**. Dark with greenish sheen (visible in good light). **Slender neck, head, pencil-thin black bill** (like flying snake). BREEDING: **White flank patch, red facial skin**. IMMATURE: Uniformly dark-brown.

Similar Species: Brandt's Cormorant (page 99) has shorter tail, band of buffy feathers at base of bill. Double-crested Cormorant (page 101) has orange facial skin, flies with crook in neck. Pelagic Cormorant slimmer overall than either, with much thinner neck, head, bill.

Seasonal Abundance: Common breeder, year-round resident in Region, especially in northern part. Ranges along both sides of North Pacific from Bering Strait to Japan, California.

Where to Find: Widespread, including waterfront in major cities. Sizeable nesting colonies on Protection, Minor Islands. Hard to miss at Point Wilson, Deception Pass State Park.

Habitat: Strictly saltwater: piers, pilings, bluffs, rocky shorelines.

Diet and Behavior: Dives deep for fish, crustaceans, other invertebrates. Has been caught in fishermen's nets at depths of 180 feet.

Voice: Grunts, croaks, groans on breeding grounds.

Did you know? Pelagic Cormorants can leap directly from the water into flight. Other cormorants must run along the surface to gain takeoff speed.

Date & Location Seen: _____

American Bittern

Green Heron

AMERICAN BITTERN / GREEN HERON
Botaurus lentiginosus / Butorides virescens

Description: 28" / 17", wingspan 42" / 26". Stocky waders, fly with neck pulled in. BITTERN: Larger, **streaked brownish**, black stripe on side of neck, **greenish legs**. Dark, pointed flight feathers contrast with back. HERON: **Small**, dark-greenish above, purplish-rufous below, white streaking at breast center, **orangish legs**; immature brown-streaked below.

Similar Species: Immature Black-crowned Night-Heron (not shown; rare in Region) similar to bittern with rounder, even-colored wings.

Seasonal Abundance: Uncommon residents in Region, rare in winter. Range across North America, winter to Central America.

Where to Find: Throughout lowlands. Nisqually National Wildlife Refuge, Montlake Fill good locations for both.

Habitat: BITTERN: Large freshwater or brackish open marshes with tall, dense vegetation. HERON: Mostly sheltered freshwater sites with trees nearby.

Diet and Behavior: Secretive, usually solitary. Forage mostly at water, primarily for fish. BITTERN: Hides with neck extended, bill pointing up; nests on ground in marsh. HERON: Nests in trees, sometimes near neighborhoods.

Voice: BITTERN: Deep pump-like *boonk ahh* song; squawks in alarm. HERON: Loud *kyow*.

Did you know? Green Herons were unknown in Washington until 1939 but have increased steadily. American Bitterns are declining across their range.

Date & Location Seen: _____

GREAT BLUE HERON
Ardea herodias

Description: 48", wingspan 72". **Long-necked**, long-legged wader with formidable **dagger-like bill**. Mostly bluish-gray above, lighter below, **white face topped with black plumes**. In flight neck usually pulled in, legs trail behind; wings broad, slightly cupped. JUVENILE, NON-BREEDING: Duller.

Similar Species: Great Egret (not shown; rare in Region) slightly smaller, all-white. Black-crowned Night-Heron (not shown; rare in Region) somewhat similar in plumage but considerably smaller with short neck, bill.

Seasonal Abundance: Common resident in Region. Ranges across North America from southern Alaska to Maritimes, south to northern South America.

Where to Find: Throughout Region.

Habitat: Marshes, ponds, estuaries, agricultural fields, rivers, lakes.

Diet and Behavior: Forages by standing or walking slowly, equally likely in water or fields. Extremely varied diet includes any animal life that can be grasped or speared with bill; rodents important component in Region. Nests primarily in colonies in tall dead or dying trees.

Voice: Loud croaking, often drawn-out *frahhhnnk*, usually given when flushed.

Did you know? Great Blue Herons may be mistaken for Sandhill Cranes (not shown; rare in Region) but are not related to the cranes, which never fly with their necks pulled in as herons do.

Date & Location Seen: _____

Description: 26", wingspan 66". Blackish, long-tailed, with small, bare **red head**; soars on long, fairly broad, two-toned **wings held above horizontal in tipping, unsteady flight**. Appears plump when perched. JUVENILE: Black head.

Similar Species: Immature Bald Eagle (page 113), Red-tailed Hawk (page 121) soar with wings held flatter; heads larger, different underwing patterns. Northern Harrier (page 115) similar in flight but rump white.

Seasonal Abundance: Fairly common but local summer resident in Region; numbers augmented by migrants, especially in fall. Arrives by March, departs by October. Ranges from southern Canada to South America.

Where to Find: Throughout Region up to mountain passes, scarce in urban areas. Best bets include Snoqualmie Valley, Enumclaw vicinity, San Juan Islands.

Habitat: Open areas such as agricultural fields, clearcuts, in proximity to forested hills.

Diet and Behavior: Soars, searching for dead animals by sight, smell. Seldom flaps, relying on thermals for soaring. Gregarious, usually roosting, migrating, feeding in groups. Reluctantly crosses water bodies in migration, waiting for favorable winds – resulting at times in concentrated migratory flights.

Voice: Grunting, hissing (seldom heard).

Did you know? Turkey Vultures often perch with wings spread and backs to the sun, for warmth. Sunshine disinfects feathers and may help restore their proper shape.

Date & Location Seen: _____

Description: 23", wingspan 63". **Blackish above** except for **whitish crown**. **Mostly-white underparts** contrast with **dark mask**, strongly-banded wings, tail. Wings long, somewhat angled (gull-like) with dark patch at wrist.

Similar Species: Immature Bald Eagle (page 113) in transitional plumage never has all-white underparts, but may show dark mask on white head. Gulls have more pointed wings.

Seasonal Abundance: Fairly common summer resident in Region, arrives late March, most depart by October but a few linger – very rarely to winter. Range worldwide; northern birds winter to southern continents.

Where to Find: Throughout Region; highest concentration at Everett waterfront.

Habitat: Usually near water including rivers, lakes, estuaries, but migrants may be far from water.

Diet and Behavior: Feeds almost exclusively on live fish, hovering over water, plunging feet-first, sometimes catching prey well below surface. Feet equipped with bumps called spicules that assist talons in holding fish. Pairs raise young on top of broken tree, power tower, platform, building bulky nest, often near human habitation. May be loosely colonial.

Voice: Noisy, calling with slurred, shrill whistles.

Did you know? This unique species, classified in a family of its own, is rebounding from severe losses resulting from DDT.

Date & Location Seen: _____

First-year

First-year

Description: 33", wingspan 82". ADULT: Dark-brown with **white head, tail**; feet, eye, huge bill yellow. Soars on **long, broad wings**. FIRST-YEAR: Lacks white head, tail; bill, eye dark. Birds transition to adult plumage, bill, eye color over four years.

Similar Species: Hawks have shorter wings. Golden Eagle (not shown; uncommon in Region) has golden feathers on nape, smaller head, bill; immature with white patches at center of wing, base of tail.

Seasonal Abundance: Common resident in Region, harder to find in early fall when disperses to north. Ranges Alaska to Labrador, south to northern Mexico.

Where to Find: Mostly lowlands; concentrates along rivers in winter (e.g., Skagit River near Rockport), later in winter to coastal flats.

Habitat: Usually near bodies of water – coastline, lakes, rivers.

Diet and Behavior: Feeds mostly on fish when available, including spawned-out salmon in rivers, also water birds, geese, carrion, other prey; steals food from smaller raptors. Pairs return to territories in mid-fall, may work on nests; eggs laid by early March, young fledge by late July.

Voice: Far-carrying call – series of chirping whistles, piercing screams.

Did you know? After breeding, many Bald Eagles in the Region track migrating salmon, moving to northern rivers for the earlier spawning runs and southern rivers for the late-fall/winter runs.

Date & Location Seen: _____

Female

Male

Description: 19", wingspan 44". Slim, **long-winged**, with **owl-like face**, long, banded tail, **white rump**. Usually flies with **wings held above horizontal**. MALE: Adult gray (whiter below) with black wingtips. FEMALE: Larger; brown above, streaked below. IMMATURE: Resembles female, but juvenile orangish on breast, lacking streaks.

Similar Species: White rump distinctive. Rough-legged Hawk (page 123) has white tail base, not rump. Red-tailed Hawk (page 121) has broader wings. Cooper's Hawk (page 119) smaller, holds wings flatter. Falcons have more pointed wings, swifter flight.

Seasonal Abundance: Locally common migrant, winter resident in Region, uncommon breeder. Ranges across northern hemisphere, winters to northern tropics. North American population sometimes considered separate species.

Where to Find: Lowlands; migrants rarely in mountains, urban areas.

Habitat: Open areas including marshes, fields, agricultural flats, occasionally clearcuts.

Diet and Behavior: Courses low, "harries" prey, using vision, hearing to locate movement, then dives to flush, catch small mammals, birds. May hover briefly. Concentrates at productive locations to hunt, roost. Nests on ground.

Voice: Calls include whistles, also rapid chatter heard while breeding, occasionally on winter quarters.

Did you know? Male Northern Harriers may mate with several females. Courting pairs perform spectacular roller-coaster flights and prey transfers high in the air.

Date & Location Seen: _____

Immature

Adult

Description: 12", wingspan 24" (averages; female larger than male). **Small**, slim, short-winged hawk with **long, matchstick-thin yellow legs**, broadly-banded, **long, square-tipped tail**. Alternates rapid flapping with gliding. ADULT: Barred reddish-brown below, head, back gray, eye bright-red. IMMATURE: Brownish back, streaked brown-and-white below. JUVENILE: Eye yellow.

Similar Species: Cooper's Hawk (page 119) nearly identical, but larger, tail rounder at tip; adult has "capped", sometimes square-headed appearance. Size separation tricky – female Sharp-shinned barely smaller than male Cooper's. American Kestrel (page 227), Merlin (page 229) have pointed wings.

Seasonal Abundance: Fairly common migrant in Region, less common in winter; uncommon breeder. Ranges from Alaska to Labrador, winters south to Central America.

Where to Find: Throughout Region.

Habitat: Breeds in dense conifer or mixed forest. Migrants, winter birds in broken woodland, brushy areas, neighborhoods.

Diet and Behavior: Feeds almost exclusively on birds, often near bird feeders. Bursts forth from hidden perch to surprise prey in low, rapid flight. Often shadows migrating songbird flocks. Pugnacious if concealed nest discovered.

Voice: Series of high-pitched *kews*.

Did you know? Many Sharp-shinned Hawks remain year round in their breeding range, but disperse widely in fall using thermals to assist travel and to locate prey while soaring.

Date & Location Seen: _____

Immature

Description: 17″, wingspan 33″ (averages; female larger than male). **Lanky**, short-winged hawk, **long, yellow, pencil-sized legs, long, broadly-banded tail**. Soars with wings held straight across. ADULT: Barred reddish-brown below, **dark-gray cap**, grayish back, pale-gray neck, eye reddish. IMMATURE: Brown back, white with brown streaks below. JUVENILE: Eye yellow.

Similar Species: Sharp-shinned Hawk (page 117) almost identical but smaller, with thinner legs, tail squarer at tip. Adult lacks "capped" appearance, soars with wrists held forward. Size separation tricky – male Cooper's only slightly larger than female Sharp-shinned. Red-tailed Hawk (page 121) lacks broad tail bands. Northern Goshawk (page 375) adult gray, immature heavily streaked to undertail.

Seasonal Abundance: Fairly common migrant, resident in Region. Secretive nester, much more evident in other seasons. Ranges across continent, southern Canada to Central America.

Where to Find: Throughout Region.

Habitat: Forest, broken woodland, farms, neighborhoods.

Diet and Behavior: Ambushes prey from hidden perch with rapid burst of speed, also cruises, searches; often stakes out bird feeders. Takes mostly birds, also small mammals while nesting. Disperses widely in fall although many remain year round in breeding range.

Voice: Calls include repeated *kek*, nasal squawks.

Did you know? Cooper's Hawks sometimes breed at one year, while still in juvenal plumage.

Date & Location Seen: _____

Immature

Description: 20", wingspan 48". Bulky. Soars on **broad wings** held flat. **Dark line on leading edge of underwing** from neck to wrist, **dark head**, streaked band across belly. ADULT: Reddish tail. IMMATURE: Brown, finely-banded tail, whiter breast. DARK MORPH: Adult brown except lighter flight feathers. HARLAN'S: Usually blackish, lacks brown tones; tail whitish.

Similar Species: Rough-legged Hawk (page 123) has white tail with black tip, whitish head, dark wrist marks on underwings, soars with wings held above horizontal. Eagles (page 113) have longer wings.

Seasonal Abundance: Most common, widespread hawk in Region, numbers augmented by migrants, wintering birds. Dark morph uncommon; Harlan's uncommon winter visitor. Ranges across North America south of tree line, to Central America.

Where to Find: Nearly anywhere.

Habitat: Open habitats, edges – highly adaptable. Fields, freeway corridors, clearcuts, open woods.

Diet and Behavior: Hunts for wide variety of prey, mostly from perch, swooping to capture prey in talons. Also soars, sometimes "kites" in stationary hover in wind. Will take carrion. Protects territory year round, calling at intruders.

Voice: Most common call rasping, down-slurred scream.

Did you know? Red-tailed Hawks come in an amazing assortment of plumages. Variation among regional populations, color morphs, ages, and even individuals can make this common species difficult to identify.

Date & Location Seen: _____

Light Morph

Immature Light Morph

Dark Morph

Description: 21″, wingspan 53″. Broad-winged, bulky, soaring hawk with **highly variable** plumage dependant on sex, age, color morph. Key marks include **white tail with wide black tip, whitish head** with dark eye-line, small bill, **white upper breast,** dark belly, white underwings with **dark wrist patches.** Less-common dark morph appears blackish except for white flight feathers contrasting with front of underwing.

Similar Species: Red-tailed Hawk (page 121) immature may appear similar, especially when hovering, but wings less pointed, held flatter; underwing lacks wrist mark, instead has dark line on leading edge.

Seasonal Abundance: Fairly common, local winter resident in Region, arrives October, departs by April. Breeds on Arctic tundra in North America, Eurasia, winters to temperate latitudes.

Where to Find: Winters in lowlands but migrants also use mountains. Good bets include Samish Flats, Nisqually National Wildlife Refuge.

Habitat: Agricultural fields, prairies, beachside dunes, marshes.

Diet and Behavior: Hunts mostly for small mammals from perch or by hovering in place; also takes birds, carrion. Soars with wings held above horizontal. Often perches on twigs that appear small for its bulk. Sometimes forms communal roosts in winter.

Voice: Seldom heard except when nesting.

Did you know? Rough-legged Hawk is the only hawk in the Puget Sound Region with feathered ("rough") legs.

Date & Location Seen: _____

Description: 10". Long-legged marsh bird with **reddish-brown breast**, gray face, **long, thin, slightly downcurved red bill**, banded black-and-white flanks, short tail (often cocked upward). JUVENILE: Smaller, more dusky.

Similar Species: Sora (not shown) has gray breast, shorter, thicker yellow bill, black face. Similar in size, behavior, habitat preferences, but scarce in Region.

Seasonal Abundance: Fairly common summer resident in Region; most leave September, return March. Uncommon winter resident. Breeds across North America from southern Canada south, except for lower Great Plains, Southeast; winters along coasts, in Mexico. Also resident in South America.

Where to Find: Anywhere in lowlands with suitable habitat, e.g., Nisqually National Wildlife Refuge, Montlake Fill.

Habitat: Pond edges, estuaries, marshes (freshwater or brackish), even roadside ditches. Needs shallow standing water, emergent vegetation, lots of edges.

Diet and Behavior: Largely animal diet – insects, larvae, snails, spiders, small frogs, small fish; some vegetal material. Probes with bill in mud, shallow water, dead vegetation. Weak flier; mostly runs or walks, staying well hidden.

Voice: Calls include *kiddik kiddik kiddik* in breeding season; series of grunts, often in duet, throughout year.

Did you know? Virginia Rails have flexible vertebrae to help them thread their way through dense standing vegetation, and long toes for walking on floating mats.

Date & Location Seen: _____

Description: 15", wingspan 26". **Dark-gray** aquatic bird, undertail edged in white. **Black head, red iris, pointed white bill with band near tip, white forehead shield** (dark-red or brown at top). Legs greenish to yellowish, **long lobed toes**. JUVENILE: Paler, legs gray, no red on forehead shield.

Similar Species: Distinctive. Pied-billed Grebe (page 91) brown.

Seasonal Abundance: Fairly common summer resident in Region, common winter resident (September–March). Nests western half of North America, Midwest; winters along coasts, in southern U.S., south to Costa Rica.

Where to Find: Widespread in lowlands. Summers wherever it finds suitable habitat. Puget Sound one of most important wintering areas; often forms large rafts. Present in all seasons in Union Bay Marsh (Lake Washington, Seattle).

Habitat: Breeds in shallow freshwater lakes, wetlands with emergent vegetation, open water. Winters on lakes, ponds, protected saltwater bays.

Diet and Behavior: Dives or tips up in shallow water, grazes on lawns, fields. Eats mostly plants, a few invertebrates. Needs long takeoff path, splashing strides on water, until airborne.

Voice: *Puck* notes singly or in series; array of other cackling, clucking, crowing calls.

Did you know? Wigeons and Gadwalls often swim with American Coots, wait for them to surface, and steal the aquatic vegetation they bring up.

Date & Location Seen: _____

Breeding

Non-breeding

Description: 11″. Plump, with **short bill**, relatively short, blackish legs. BREEDING: Adults show **black face, breast, belly**, whitish crown, neck, sides, undertail, spangled back. Female, molting birds browner, less distinctly marked. NON-BREEDING: Speckled brownish-gray above with indistinct whitish eyebrow, plainer below; **black armpits** visible in flight. JUVENILE: Browner with grayish legs.

Similar Species: Distinctive in breeding plumage, bill shorter than other large shorebirds. American, Pacific Golden-Plovers (neither shown; both rare in Region) slightly smaller, more golden in summer; browner, lack black armpit in fall.

Seasonal Abundance: Fairly common migrant, winter resident in Region. Breeds on Arctic tundra around northern hemisphere, winters to southern continents.

Where to Find: Lowlands, mostly coastal; locally common on Skagit, Samish Flats. Rare in urbanized areas, especially southern part of Region.

Habitat: Mudflats, short-grass or plowed fields, beaches, open marsh.

Diet and Behavior: Forages visually by running, stopping, picking food from ground; also may probe. Diet mostly worms, insects, marine organisms. Birds spread out to feed but roost in groups, often flocking with other shorebirds, especially Dunlin.

Voice: Very vocal. Most common call forlorn-sounding, whistled *plee o weee*.

Did you know? This widespread species is known in Eurasia as the Gray Plover.

Date & Location Seen: _____

Description: 7". Plain grayish-brown above except for **white-and-black collar, forehead**, black cheek; **white below with black breast band. Bill short** with pinkish-orange base; pinkish-yellow legs short. White wing stripe on long wings visible in flight. JUVENILE: Duller with dark bill.

Similar Species: Shorter bill separates from sandpipers. Killdeer (page 133) larger with double breast band; juvenile Killdeer usually appears fluffy.

Seasonal Abundance: Fairly common but local migrant in Region, arrives mid-July, most gone by October. Returns late April–May. Breeds across North American Arctic, subarctic, winters as far south as South America.

Where to Find: Lowlands; more common in northern parts of Region. Good spots include Whidbey Island, Fir Island.

Habitat: Wide-open places; prefers marine environments such as tideflats, mudflats, beaches. Also agricultural fields (flooded, plowed), pond margins.

Diet and Behavior: Forages visually by running, stopping, picking food from ground. Feeds on marine organisms, insects. Usually in flocks, associates loosely with other shorebirds.

Voice: Common flight call whistled *chu wee*. Trills, chatters during interactions with others of its species.

Did you know? Semipalmated Plover gets its name from its partially-webbed feet.

Date & Location Seen: _____

Description: 10". Plain brown above with white collar, **white below except for two black breast bands**. Forehead, eyebrow white; **bill dark, short**; legs relatively short, yellowish. **Orange tail, rump**, white wing stripe visible in flight. Scarlet eye-ring. JUVENILE: One breast band when half-grown.

Similar Species: Semipalmated Plover (page 131) smaller with one breast band, shorter bill, lacks orange rump.

Seasonal Abundance: Common summer resident in Region, less common in winter. Ranges from Alaska, Newfoundland to South America; withdraws from coldest areas in winter.

Where to Find: Mostly lowlands, also up major river valleys to moderate elevations.

Habitat: Open habitats without high grass: lawns, road edges, beaches, mudflats, plowed fields, parking lots. Prefers bare gravel near water for nesting.

Diet and Behavior: Forages visually by running, stopping, picking food from ground. Feeds mostly on insects, also some seeds. Secretive at open nest site but calls, feigns broken wing as part of distraction display when discovered. Flocks concentrate in farm fields in late summer.

Voice: Varied strident calls include *kill deeah, deee*, and *dee ahy*. Gives high, rapid trill when nervous.

Did you know? The Killdeer's four black-spotted green eggs are nearly invisible in their gravel nest when left unattended.

Date & Location Seen: _____

_____

Description: 17". **Chunky, all-black** shorebird with long, chisel-like, **bright-red bill**, eye-ring. Pinkish-yellow, relatively short legs, golden eye. JUVENILE: Duller, with dark-tipped, dull-red bill.

Similar Species: None in Region.

Seasonal Abundance: Uncommon resident in Region. Ranges along Pacific Coast from southern Alaska to Baja California.

Where to Find: Limited to rocky coastline in northern part of Region. Good spots include San Juan Islands, Ediz Hook, John Wayne Marina in Sequim Bay, Deception Pass State Park.

Habitat: Rocky shores, islets, cobble beaches, jetties, breakwaters.

Diet and Behavior: Forages mostly when tide low, primarily for mussels, other shellfish. Uses laterally-compressed bill to pry shells apart. Also feeds on other marine organisms. Usually in pairs or family groups, but also forms small flocks outside breeding season. Non-migratory, but disperses infrequently to coastal localities away from nesting grounds. May roost with bill tucked under wing – less easily identified then.

Voice: Loud, ringing yelps, whistles; rolling series given in display.

Did you know? A lost Black Oystercatcher was found in distress in January 1947 at over 3,000 feet elevation in the Cascades in Yakima County!

Date & Location Seen: _____

Breeding

Non-breeding

Description: 8". Small, with **short reddish bill**, short yellowish legs, **white wing stripe** visible in flight, white eye-line, **constant teetering motion**. BREEDING: **Dark spots** on white underparts, bill brighter red. NON-BREEDING: Evenly grayish-brown above to dusky neck; **white underparts extend up side in front of folded wing**. JUVENILE: White edges on wing feathers.

Similar Species: Solitary Sandpiper (not shown; rare in Region) also teeters; taller, with greenish legs, fine white back spotting, strong white eye-ring, lacks black eye-line.

Seasonal Abundance: Fairly common summer resident in Region; rare in winter. Ranges across North America, winters to South America.

Where to Find: Widespread, from lowlands to mountains.

Habitat: Nests along ponds, rivers, mountain streams, other fresh water in open or wooded terrain. Frequents pebbly pond edges, coastline, mudflats, sewage ponds at other seasons.

Diet and Behavior: Forages visually by picking, chasing, fluttering after insects, small organisms, tiny fish; may take carrion. Highly territorial at all seasons so does not flock. Distinctive flapping flight: short pulses with wings not raised above horizontal, alternating with glides on bowed wings.

Voice: Loud, repeated, clear, high-pitched whistles.

Did you know? Spotted Sandpiper is one of a small number of shorebird species where females sometimes mate with more than one male.

Date & Location Seen: _____

**Greater Yellowlegs
Breeding**

**Greater Yellowlegs
Juvenile**

**Lesser Yellowlegs
Breeding**

**Lesser Yellowlegs
Juvenile**

Description: 14" / 10". Elegant, grayish waders with **long, bright-yellowish-orange legs**, long neck, fairly long, mostly dark bill, whitish speckling on dark back. Lighter below, with **plain wings, white rump** visible in flight. Breast streaked in breeding plumage. GREATER: More robust, thicker legs, **bill longer, slightly upturned**, pale-based. LESSER: More **delicate; bill shorter, straighter**.

Similar Species: Solitary Sandpiper (not shown; rare in Region) slightly smaller than Lesser, with greenish legs, white eye-ring.

Seasonal Abundance: Fairly common migrants in Region. GREATER: Arrives July, a few linger in winter; returns March–May. Breeds southern Alaska to Labrador, winters to South America. LESSER: Arrives by July, departs by October, rarely winters; uncommon in spring. Breeds Alaska to central Canada, winters to South America.

Where to Find: Lowlands.

Habitat: Flooded fields, marshes, ponds, estuaries, tideflats. LESSER: Less likely in saltwater habitat.

Diet and Behavior: Forage in shallow water, swinging bill side to side or running after small fish, insects, other organisms; often flock, sometimes with other shorebirds.

Voice: Call *tew*, repeated 3–4 times in GREATER, 2–3 times in LESSER; both *tew* continuously in alarm.

Did you know? Greater Yellowlegs has nested in Oregon, 500 miles south of its normal breeding range.

Date & Location Seen: _____

Description: 17". **Large**, with long, grayish legs, **long, downcurved bill, bold brown-and-buff head stripes**. Overall grayish-brown with whitish belly; back mottled, streaked. All plumages similar.

Similar Species: Long-billed Curlew (not shown; rare in Region) even larger, longer-billed, with cinnamon underwings (barred brownish in Whimbrel). Marbled, Bar-tailed Godwits (neither shown; both rare in Region) similar in size with long, upturned bill.

Seasonal Abundance: Fairly common spring, uncommon fall migrant in Region, rare winter resident. Late spring migrants pass through in early June, earliest fall birds return later that month. Breeds around northern hemisphere on Arctic tundra, winters coastally to tropics.

Where to Find: Lowlands; quite local. Skagit Flats, Nisqually National Wildlife Refuge good bets for spring migrant flocks; fall coastal sites include Ediz Hook, Dungeness.

Habitat: Plowed agricultural fields, mudflats, rocky shores, marshes, meadows.

Diet and Behavior: Forages by walking, picks or probes just below surface for worms, crabs, other invertebrates; may eat some plant material. Large spring flocks drawn to newly-plowed fields; fall migrants alone or in smaller groups may flock with other shorebirds, usually at coast.

Voice: Common call loud *whi whi whi whi whi* whistle, also other trills, whistles in spring.

Did you know? The Eurasian race of the Whimbrel has a white rump.

Date & Location Seen: _____

Ruddy Turnstone
Breeding

Breeding

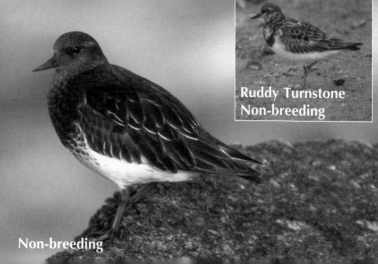

Ruddy Turnstone
Non-breeding

Non-breeding

Description: 9″. Stocky with brownish legs, short, **black, chisel-like bill, black tail with white base. White back, wing stripe, underwing, shoulder patch visible in flight**. BREEDING: Black above; white patches above, below eye; white belly. NON-BREEDING: Browner above, without face markings. JUVENILE: As non-breeding.

Similar Species: Larger Surfbird (page 145) lacks white back patches in flight. **Ruddy Turnstone** (see insets; less common in Region) has **reddish legs, harlequin pattern** (rufous-black-white) in breeding plumage; dull-brown in winter.

Seasonal Abundance: Fairly common migrant, winter resident in Region from mid-July through April. Breeds coastal Alaskan tundra, winters on coast from southeastern Alaska to Mexico.

Where to Find: Coastline. Local; good spots include Ediz Hook, Penn Cove, West Seattle.

Habitat: Rocky shores, breakwaters, log booms, occasionally beaches, mudflats.

Diet and Behavior: Forages on rocks, prying off mussels, other marine organisms; also turns rocks, shells to search beneath; may feed on carrion, plant material. Roosts, feeds in flocks, often with other shorebirds, particularly Surfbirds.

Voice: Highly vocal, with shrill rattles, chatter – especially when flushed.

Did you know? More wary than Surfbirds, Black Turnstones act as sentinels for both species, calling frequently in alarm.

Date & Location Seen: _____

Non-breeding

Non-breeding

Description: 10″. Dark, **stocky**, with short yellowish legs, **short chisel-like bill** (black with yellow base), broad white wing stripe, **white tail with broad black band at tip**. BREEDING: Rufous highlights on back feathers; heavily marked with dark chevrons on white belly, flanks. NON-BREEDING: Evenly grayish-brown with fewer marks on belly. JUVENILE: May appear browner.

Similar Species: Black Turnstone (page 143) smaller with white on back, inner wing. Sandpipers have longer bills.

Seasonal Abundance: Fairly common fall migrant, winter resident in Region (mid-July–April). Breeds on alpine tundra of Alaska, Yukon, winters on Pacific Coast from Alaska south to Chile.

Where to Find: Coastline. Very local in Region; good spots include Port Townsend, Penn Cove on Whidbey Island, West Seattle.

Habitat: Rocky shores, jetties, breakwaters, rarely on sand or mudflats.

Diet and Behavior: Forages by pulling mussels, barnacles, other marine organisms from rocks. Roosts, feeds in flocks, almost always with other rock-loving shorebirds, particularly Black Turnstones. Often allows close approach.

Voice: Seldom vocal in Region; occasional high squeaks, chatter.

Did you know? The nesting grounds of the Surfbird on remote ridgetops and mountains remained undiscovered until the 1920s.

Date & Location Seen: _____

Breeding

Non-breeding

Description: 7¹/₂". Small but **stout**, with black, relatively short, **straight, blunt-tipped bill**, short **black legs**. In flight, broad **white wing stripe** contrasts with dark flight feathers. BREEDING: Upperparts **rufous**, underparts white. NON-BREEDING: **Pale-gray above** with clean white underparts. JUVENILE: Upperparts more spangled with blackish, may show some buff below.

Similar Species: Other small shorebirds darker than Sanderling in non-breeding plumage. Bright breeding plumage unique (seen only late spring in Region).

Seasonal Abundance: Fairly common migrant, winter resident in Region (August–May). Breeds on high Arctic tundra around northern hemisphere, winters from Alaska to southernmost parts of southern continents.

Where to Find: Coastal; rare away from salt water. Good bets include Dungeness, Discovery Park.

Habitat: Beaches, sometimes mudflats.

Diet and Behavior: Actively forages on beach just above waves, running with legs moving rapidly like wind-up toy. Picks, probes for small marine organisms on sand or mud, may eat some carrion. Roosts, feeds in flocks, sometimes with other shorebirds.

Voice: Most common call sharp *kip*.

Did you know? Sanderlings that winter in the southern hemisphere may fly over 8,000 miles each year to reach their nesting grounds in spring.

Date & Location Seen: _____

Breeding

Non-breeding

Juvenile

Description: 6¹/₄″. Small sandpiper, brownish-gray with evenly-tapered, **drooping, fine-tipped bill, blackish legs**, white belly, whitish eye-line; thin white wing stripe visible in flight. BREEDING: **Rufous highlights in back, head feathers**, black chevron marks on flanks. NON-BREEDING: Evenly grayish-brown with white underparts. JUVENILE: Paler, less strongly marked than breeding adult.

Similar Species: : Semipalmated Sandpiper (not shown; rare in Region) has blunt, short bill, little or no rufous coloring. Baird's Sandpiper (not shown; uncommon fall migrant in Region) slightly larger with thin, straight bill, folded wings longer than tail. Sanderling (page 147) larger, with shorter, blunt bill. Least Sandpiper (page 151) has yellowish legs.

Seasonal Abundance: Common migrant in Region July–November; a few winter. Breeding-plumaged flocks present spring, early summer. Breeds Alaska west to Siberia, winters coastally to South America.

Where to Find: Throughout lowlands, mostly coastal.

Habitat: Open shoreline, mudflats, muddy fields, tidal estuaries.

Diet and Behavior: Probes, picks small organisms from mud while wading, walking; may eat seeds. Feeds, roosts in flocks with other shorebirds.

Voice: Flight call thin *dcheet*. Feeding flocks may chatter.

Did you know? Western Sandpiper is the most abundant migrant shorebird in western Washington. Spring counts at Grays Harbor, on the outer coast, have exceeded a half million in a day!

Date & Location Seen: _____

Breeding

Non-breeding

Juvenile

Description: 5½″. **Smallest sandpiper**, brownish with **short, fine-tipped, drooping bill, yellowish legs, brownish upper breast,** white belly, white lines down back; thin white wing stripe visible in flight. BREEDING: Darker with black centers on back feathers. NON-BREEDING: Evenly grayish-brown with whitish belly. JUVENILE: More rufous than adult, legs duller.

Similar Species: Western Sandpiper (page 149), Baird's Sandpiper (not shown; uncommon fall migrant in Region) have black legs. Baird's larger with thin, straight bill. Pectoral Sandpiper (not shown; uncommon migrant in Region) similar but much larger, legs proportionally longer.

Seasonal Abundance: Common migrant in Region July–October, less common April–May. A few winter. Breeds Alaska–Labrador, winters to northern South America.

Where to Find: Throughout Region, mostly in lowlands.

Habitat: Mudflats, pond margins, marshes, coastal bays, muddy pools, ditches.

Diet and Behavior: Forages mostly by picking, sometimes probing, primarily for insects, aquatic organisms; may eat some plant material. Frequently in small groups rather than large flocks. Not shy, often allowing close approach.

Voice: Flight call *pree eet*. Birds may utter *dee dee dee* call among themselves.

Did you know? The small North American sandpipers (including Least and Western) are often referred to collectively as "peeps", together with the stints of Eurasia.

Date & Location Seen: _____

Breeding

Non-breeding

DUNLIN
Calidris alpina

Description: 8½". Fairly small, **hunched appearance**, with **short, dark legs, long, dark bill with drooping tip**; white wing stripe visible in flight. BREEDING: Spring birds mostly **rufous above with black belly**, whitish face, upper breast. NON-BREEDING: **Plain brownish-gray** with white belly, underwing, faint eye-line.

Similar Species: Larger with longer bill than other small shorebirds. Smaller size, drooping bill separate Dunlin from dowitchers (page 155).

Seasonal Abundance: Common migrant, winter resident in Region, arrives late in fall (mostly October). Attains breeding plumage by April, departs by early May. Breeds on tundra around northern hemisphere, winters south from temperate latitudes to subtropics.

Where to Find: Throughout lowlands; most common in northern part of Region, where flocks number in tens of thousands.

Habitat: Coastal bays, tidal flats, muddy fields, rarely far from salt water.

Diet and Behavior: Forages by picking, probing mud, primarily for aquatic organisms; may eat some plant material. Tight, swirling flocks move with mechanized precision, alternately flashing white, gray; large numbers in distance may appear to be smoke.

Voice: Flight call harsh *kreev*.

Did you know? Formerly known as Red-backed Sandpiper in reference to its bright spring color, the Dunlin derives its current name from the "dun" plumage it wears for most of the year.

Date & Location Seen: _____

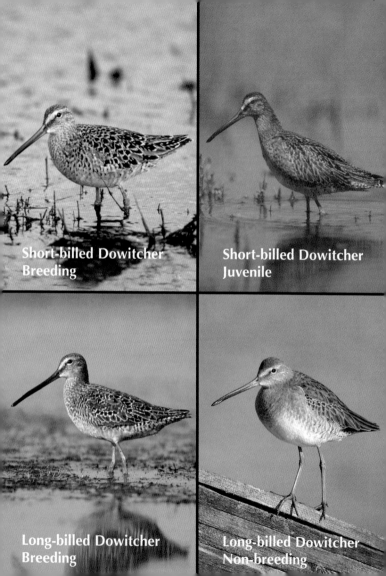

Short-billed Dowitcher
Breeding

Short-billed Dowitcher
Juvenile

Long-billed Dowitcher
Breeding

Long-billed Dowitcher
Non-breeding

Description: 11". Stocky. **Long, straight bill, white wedge on back**, finely-banded tail, greenish legs, mostly dark wings, **whitish eye-line. Rusty breast in breeding plumage**, overall grayish in winter. SHORT-BILLED: Summer–fall juvenile has **bright-golden markings near tip of folded wing**. LONG-BILLED: Underparts entirely rusty in breeding plumage (Short-billed has white belly).

Similar Species: Longer bill than similarly-sized shorebirds except Wilson's Snipe (page 157) which has white stripes on head, back. Stilt Sandpiper (not shown; rare fall migrant in Region) smaller, proportionally longer-legged, may feed with dowitchers.

Seasonal Abundance: Fairly common migrants in Region. SHORT-BILLED: Arrives late June, departs by October, back April–May. Breeds Canada, Alaska, winters to South America. LONG-BILLED: Arrives July, a few winter; numbers increase May. Breeds northwestern North America, northeastern Siberia, winters to Mexico.

Where to Find: Throughout lowlands.

Habitat: Mudflats, marshes, pools. SHORT-BILLED prefers tideflats, LONG-BILLED fresh water.

Diet and Behavior: Probe mud like sewing machine, primarily for aquatic organisms, also plant material. Usually flock, often with other shorebirds.

Voice: SHORT-BILLED: Low, liquid, whistled *tlu tu tu*, given in flight. LONG-BILLED: Sharp *keek*, sometimes in rapid series.

Did you know? The two species are difficult to separate. Bill length averages longer for Long-billed but there is much overlap.

Date & Location Seen: _____

Description: 10". Stocky. Mostly brown with **long, straight bill**, short, greenish legs, dark wings, **rust-orange tail, white lower breast, belly**. Bold **whitish streaks on head, face, back**, dark bars along flanks.

Similar Species: Much longer bill than other similarly-sized shorebirds except dowitchers (page 155), which lack white stripes on head, back.

Seasonal Abundance: Fairly common migrant, winter resident in Region (July–May); rare breeder. Ranges across North America, winters to northern South America.

Where to Find: Throughout lowlands, up to moderate elevations.

Habitat: Wet ground including marshes, bogs, flooded fields, margins of ponds, streams.

Diet and Behavior: Forages mostly for insects, worms, other organisms by probing mud, shallow water. Sits tight, relying on camouflage until approached closely, then flushes explosively. Often concentrates in loose flocks during migration. Male flies high in breeding display, with shallow dives during which vibrating tail feathers produce hollow whinny sound ("winnowing").

Voice: Abrupt rasping *skresh* uttered when flushed. Breeding call *chip a*, repeated many times from exposed perch.

Did you know? The eyes of the Wilson's Snipe are set well back on the sides of the head, enabling it literally to watch its back for danger even as it probes for food.

Date & Location Seen: _____

Female Breeding

Juvenile

Description: 7¼". Small, **swimming shorebird** with straight, thin, black bill; white wing stripe visible in flight. BREEDING: Female with gray cap, white chin, reddish neck, gold-striped back, gray sides, white belly. Male similar but duller. NON-BREEDING: Gray-and-white-striped above, plain white below, with dark cap, **thick, dark line behind eye**. JUVENILE: Resembles adult non-breeding; early juveniles have gold-striped back.

Similar Species: Wilson's Phalarope (not shown; rare in Region): dark stripe extends from bill down side of neck, no wing stripe; more likely on land.

Seasonal Abundance: Fairly common fall migrant in Region, late July–October (juveniles, non-breeding-plumaged adults); less common spring migrant, mostly May (breeding-plumaged birds). Breeds on tundra at low latitudes around northern hemisphere, winters in tropical oceans. Migrates primarily at sea.

Where to Find: Local; more common in northern part of Region.

Habitat: Salt water, less often fresh water including sewage ponds, flooded fields.

Diet and Behavior: Feeds on open water while swimming, often in circles, picking insects, other small organisms from surface. Seldom occurs on land except while nesting.

Voice: Frequent *kit kit* call.

Did you know? The usual sexual roles are reversed in phalaropes, with the smaller, duller-plumaged male incubating the eggs and raising the young.

Date & Location Seen: _____

Breeding

Non-breeding

Immature

Description: 13″, wingspan 32″. **Petite**, tern-like in flight. White below, pearl-gray back, black bill, short red legs. Square tail, **upper surface of forewing white**, outer trailing edge black. BREEDING: **Head black**. NON-BREEDING: **Head white with black spot behind eye**. IMMATURE: Black tail tip, wing pattern.

Similar Species: Common Tern (page 177) has strongly-forked tail, black limited to cap. Franklin's Gull (not shown; rare in Region) larger with darker back; juveniles, non-breeding-plumaged birds show dark half-hood.

Seasonal Abundance: Common migrant in Region. Spring birds peak March–April, continue through June; fall movement begins by July, peaks October–November. Good numbers winter, so present year round. Breeds northern North America, winters to Mexico.

Where to Find: Throughout lowlands, mostly near coast; migrants also along rivers, rarely at higher elevations.

Habitat: Mostly coastal habitats, sewage lagoons; also rivers, lakes.

Diet and Behavior: Forages for small fish, crustaceans, insects by plunge-diving or picking at water surface. Concentrates, occasionally in flocks of thousands, at sewage ponds, tidal rips.

Voice: Call unlike that of most gulls – low, harsh, grating *geerr*.

Did you know? Bonaparte's Gulls build their nests in coniferous trees in the boreal forests of Alaska and Canada.

Date & Location Seen: _____

Breeding

First-year

Parasitic Jaeger

Description: 19", wingspan 49". Medium-sized, **dark, unstreaked** gull. BREEDING: White head, **red bill**, light-gray rump, underparts, **black tail with white tip**. NON-BREEDING: Head gray. FIRST-YEAR: Uniform dark-brown with yellowish, black-tipped bill. Sub-adults transition to full adult plumage over three years.

Similar Species: Distinctive in Region. Other adult gulls white below, immatures streaked or mottled. **Parasitic Jaeger** (see inset; uncommon fall migrant in Region, winters at sea) **falcon-like**; plumage variable but always with **white wing flash near tip**; harasses Bonaparte's Gulls, Common Terns in flight to steal food.

Seasonal Abundance: Fairly common summer visitor in Region (June–October), rare in other seasons. Breeds mainly Gulf of California, disperses along coast to Guatemala, British Columbia.

Where to Find: Strictly coastal. Most common San Juan Islands, less so farther south.

Habitat: Marine habitats along coast; shuns fresh water.

Diet and Behavior: Forages mostly in flight over water for fish, small marine organisms; picks from surface or makes shallow dives. Gregarious. Moves en masse along coast after nesting.

Voice: Calls more nasal, hollow than those of other gulls.

Did you know? Gulls, including Heermann's, sometimes practice kleptoparasitism (stealing food from other birds). Jaegers – close relatives of gulls – feed almost exclusively by this strategy when away from their northern breeding grounds.

Date & Location Seen: _____

Breeding

Non-breeding

Description: 15", wingspan 43". Small gull with white, **dove-like head, short yellowish bill**. BREEDING: **Dark eye**; yellow legs; white tail, underparts; light-slaty-gray back. **Wingtips black with large white spots** near tip. NON-BREEDING: Head heavily streaked. FIRST-YEAR: Streaky-brown with pink legs. Adult plumage attained in three years. Second-year bird resembles adult with black tail tip, ring near end of bill.

Similar Species: Smaller than most gulls in Region. Darker gray, more white in wingtips than Ring-billed (page 167).

Seasonal Abundance: Common winter resident in Region, arrives beginning in August, leaves by May. Breeds Alaska, northwestern Canada, winters southern Alaska to Baja California along Pacific Coast. Several other races in Eurasia.

Where to Find: Lowlands, mostly near coast, e.g., Stillaguamish, Nooksack valleys.

Habitat: Coastal habitats, rivers (especially near mouths), lakes, sewage lagoons, agricultural fields.

Diet and Behavior: Omnivorous; forages for worms in plowed fields; fish, marine organisms in coastal areas; insect larvae, waste in sewage ponds. May flycatch during insect hatches. Gregarious; often flocks with other gulls, especially Ring-billeds.

Voice: Calls higher than those of other gulls, with mewed quality.

Did you know? Although it nests on Vancouver Island at the doorstep of the Puget Sound Region, there are no breeding records of Mew Gull in Washington (so far!).

Date & Location Seen: _____

Non-breeding

Description: 17", wingspan 46". **Medium-sized** gull, pearl-gray back, white head, underparts, tail; **wingtips extensively black with white spot near tip.** BREEDING: **Yellow bill with black ring near tip,** yellow eye, legs. NON-BREEDING: Head streaked. FIRST-YEAR: Streaky-brown with dark eye, pink legs. Sub-adults transition to full adult plumage over three years.

Similar Species: Larger gulls have heavier bills. Mew Gull (page 165) has smaller bill, darker back, whiter wingtips.

Seasonal Abundance: Common resident in Region although rarely nests. Ranges from southeastern Alaska to Labrador, south to Mexico, Caribbean.

Where to Find: Throughout lowlands, rare at higher elevations.

Habitat: Coastal habitats, freshwater bodies, agricultural fields, urban settings including parking lots.

Diet and Behavior: Omnivorous. Forages widely for worms in plowed fields; crustaceans, fish in coastal areas; refuse, scraps in cities. Often flycatches during insect hatches, steals food from other birds. Long-lived, colonial nester with elaborate courtship, complex social behaviors. Gregarious, often flocks with other gulls.

Voice: Typical gull calls including long sequence of laugh-like squeals, beginning with long calls then trailing to shorter ones.

Did you know? Other gull species have rings on their bills during winter and in transitional plumages. Take care not to confuse them with Ring-billed Gulls.

Date & Location Seen: _____

Breeding

Non-breeding

Description: 20″, wingspan 53″. Fairly large gull. BREEDING: White head, underparts, tail; **light-slaty-gray back; wingtips black** with white near tip. Dark eye, **greenish-yellow legs**, fairly thin **bill with black-and-red spot near tip**. NON-BREEDING: Head streaked. FIRST-YEAR: Dark, streaky-brown (variable). Sub-adults transition to full adult plumage over four years.

Similar Species: Only gull in Region with yellowish legs, black-and-red spot on bill.

Seasonal Abundance: Uncommon winter–spring in Region, becomes fairly common by summer, locally common late summer–fall as migrants arrive from breeding colonies in eastern Washington, Great Plains. Breeds interior western North America, winters coastally British Columbia–Mexico.

Where to Find: Primarily lowlands, but may be seen flying west over mountain passes in summer.

Habitat: Mostly coastal; also lakes, rivers, farms, cities.

Diet and Behavior: Forages in coastal areas for fish, carrion, sometimes far from shore; in plowed fields for rodents, worms; in city refuse. May flycatch, steal food from other birds. Often flocks with other gulls.

Voice: Typical for gull; can be harsh.

Did you know? California Gulls rescued Mormon settlers at the Great Salt Lake from the grasshopper plague of 1848.

Date & Location Seen: _____

Breeding

Non-breeding

Description: 23", wingspan 55". Medium-large gull. BREEDING: Underparts, tail white, gray back, **wingtips appear all-gray from below** but blackish with white tips from above. Round head, **dark eye** (pale in small percentage), **small bill** with red spot, **legs bright-pink**. NON-BREEDING: **Head heavily streaked**. FIRST-YEAR: Variably mottled brown, bill black. Sub-adults transition to full adult plumage over four years.

Similar Species: Dark wingtips of other gulls apparent from below as well as from above. Herring Gull (not shown; scarce in Region) has yellow eye. Adult California Gull (page 169) has greenish-yellow legs. Hybrid Glaucous-winged x Western Gulls (page 173) may be similar, but bill much heavier, forehead sloping.

Seasonal Abundance: Fairly common winter resident in Region, arrives by October, departs March. Breeds in central Canadian Arctic; most winter along Pacific Coast, southeastern Alaska–Baja California.

Where to Find: Local. Best spots Ediz Hook, mouth of Puyallup River in industrial Tacoma.

Habitat: Primarily coastal, especially estuaries. Also ponds, fields, lots.

Diet and Behavior: Omnivorous. Forages mostly for fish, mollusks, carrion, urban refuse. Gregarious, often flocking with other gulls.

Voice: Typical for gull.

Did you know? Thayer's Gull, once classified as a race of the Herring Gull, is highly sought after by visiting bird watchers due to its relative abundance in the Region.

Date & Location Seen: _____

Western Gull

Breeding

First-year

Description: 25", wingspan 58". Large. BREEDING: White head, underparts, tail, pearl-gray back; **wingtips same gray as back**, white spots near tip. **Massive yellow bill** with red spot near tip, **pink legs**. NON-BREEDING: Head streaked. FIRST-YEAR: Streaky-brown. Sub-adults transition to full adult plumage over four years.

Similar Species: Most gulls smaller with smaller bills; other large gulls have black wingtips, except Glaucous Gull (not shown; rare in Region) which has white wingtips.

Seasonal Abundance: Common resident in Region. Range coastal (Alaska–Mexico).

Where to Find: Primarily coastal, but also inland on fresh water throughout lowlands.

Habitat: Marine habitats, including rocky shores, beaches. Also lowland lakes, rivers, cities.

Diet and Behavior: Omnivorous, opportunistic. Forages on land, water for fish, mollusks, carrion in coastal areas, refuse in cities, worms in fields. Nests in pairs on cliffs, pilings, roofs, other structures. Gregarious, flocking with other gulls.

Voice: Calls, typical for gull, include sequences of laugh-like bugling, staccato *ca ca ca* given in alarm.

Did you know? Glaucous-winged Gull hybridizes with the more southerly **Western Gull** (see inset; uncommon in Region), which is dark-gray above with black wingtips. The resulting offspring are intermediate in plumage. Many "Glaucous-wingeds" in the Puget Sound Region are actually hybrids, with wingtips a shade darker than the back.

Date & Location Seen: _____

Breeding

Description: 20″, wingspan 48″. Stocky tern, white below, pearl-gray back with large, **thick red bill, black cap**, whitish, shallowly-forked tail, **long, pointed wings** with dark tips on undersurface. NON-BREEDING: Whitish forehead. JUVENILE: Whitish forehead, back mottled with brown.

Similar Species: Common Tern (page 177) much smaller, bill thin. Except for Heermann's (page 163), gulls lack red bill.

Seasonal Abundance: Fairly common summer resident in Region (April–September). Ranges nearly worldwide in temperate, tropical zones.

Where to Find: Throughout lowlands, but local. In recent years colonies have appeared in urban areas (Tacoma, Bellingham, Everett).

Habitat: Coastal habitats, rivers, lakes. Nests in isolated pairs or large colonies, uses open sites including recently-disturbed ground, dredge-spoil islands, rooftops, undisturbed lots.

Diet and Behavior: Forages fairly high over salt or fresh water, plunge-dives for small fish, often several feet below surface; also picks fish off surface. Carries fish in bill back to nest. Colony locations may shift year to year depending on disturbance.

Voice: Often heard before seen. Common call low, harsh, screeching *kaa yarrr*. Juveniles beg with whistled *wheee oo*.

Did you know? Caspian Terns have recently come into conflict with fisheries management goals due to their skill at catching salmon smolts swimming downriver to the sea from the hatcheries where they were reared.

Date & Location Seen: _____

Description: 13″, wingspan 30″. **Slim, elegant,** white below with pearl-gray back, **black cap,** thin, black-tipped red bill, short, reddish legs. **Tail strongly forked,** white with dark edges; **wings long, pointed** with dark wedge at tip on upper surface. JUVENILE: Black bill, white forehead.

Similar Species: Caspian Tern (page 175) much larger with thick bill. Bonaparte's Gull (page 161) has square tail, white stripe on forewing. Arctic Tern, Forster's Tern (neither shown; both rare in Region) difficult to separate from Common.

Seasonal Abundance: Fairly common migrant, mostly late summer–fall. Range worldwide except Antarctica.

Where to Find: Locally on marine waters throughout Region. Best bets Point No Point, Discovery Park, Sequim Bay.

Habitat: Limited in Region to coastal waters, although elsewhere also uses freshwater habitats. Often concentrates near tidal rips, roosts on beaches, piers, boats.

Diet and Behavior: Forages for small fish by flying low over water, hovering, plunge-diving to catch prey with bill. Gregarious, often flocks with small gulls.

Voice: Calls include clipped *kip,* harsh but musical, slurred *kee ahrr.*

Did you know? Common Terns migrate through Washington on their way to and from their Arctic breeding grounds and the oceanic waters off South America where they winter.

Date & Location Seen: _____

Breeding

Non-breeding

COMMON MURRE
Uria aalge

Description: 16", wingspan 27". In all plumages, **back, crown black** (actually dark-brown), **breast, underparts white, bill long, straight, black**. BREEDING: Entire head, throat black (plumage held for much of winter). NON-BREEDING: White extends across throat, lower face to nape, with **dark line curving down behind eye**. IMMATURE: Resembles non-breeding adult.

Similar Species: Size (largest alcid in Region), solid-black back, upperwing, long bill separate it from non-breeding Marbled, Ancient Murrelets (page 183), Pigeon Guillemot (page 181).

Seasonal Abundance: Fairly common winter resident on marine waters in Region; abundance varies year to year. Nests on steep seaside cliffs in Arctic, temperate zones throughout northern hemisphere, including Washington's outer coast. Most birds winter at sea.

Where to Find: Good places include Strait of Juan de Fuca (Dungeness Spit, San Juan Islands, Port Townsend), Rosario Strait, Tacoma Narrows.

Habitat: Mostly open marine waters with strong tidal flow.

Diet and Behavior: Dives for fish, squid, crustaceans. Congregates at good feeding sites.

Voice: Silent away from breeding colonies.

Did you know? Commons Murres routinely dive to 200 feet, propelling themselves with small wings adapted for underwater swimming. In the air, however, they must beat their wings in a rapid blur to keep their two-pound bodies aloft.

Date & Location Seen: _____

Breeding

Non-breeding

PIGEON GUILLEMOT
Cepphus columba

Description: 13", wingspan 23". Bill thin, straight, black; **legs, mouth lining vermilion red**. BREEDING: **Mostly black** (actually dark-brown) except upper surface of forewing largely white – when wing folded, appears as **large white patch with black slash on lower edge**. NON-BREEDING: **Mostly white** with mottled back, dark line behind eye; white wing patch, dark wingtips retained. JUVENILE: Resembles non-breeding adult, but duskier.

Similar Species: In flight, White-winged Scoter (page 61) shows white speculum (trailing edge of wing); Pigeon Guillemot's white patch is on forewing.

Seasonal Abundance: Fairly common year-round resident in Region. Ranges along both coasts of North Pacific Ocean from Bering Strait south to California, Kurile Islands.

Where to Find: Widely distributed on marine waters. In winter, concentrates more in good feeding areas (Tacoma Narrows, Budd Inlet, Sequim Bay, Rosario Strait).

Habitat: Exclusively saltwater. Nests in crevices along shoreline, including breakwaters, jetties – in Washington, mostly in burrows in bluffs. Forages in relatively shallow, protected waters.

Diet and Behavior: Takes small fish, shrimp, crabs, other organisms, at surface or by diving.

Voice: Trills, whistles given near nest.

Did you know? Winter numbers increase in the Puget Sound Region as Pigeon Guillemots move north from California and abandon the outer coast.

Date & Location Seen: _____

Breeding

Ancient Murrelet

Non-breeding

Description: 10″, wingspan 16″. Compact, short-necked alcid with **small, dark bill**. BREEDING: Brownish. Head, wings dark, body **"marbled" brown-and-buffy**. NON-BREEDING: Black upperparts, white flanks, **white streak where wings join back**. White chin, throat, collar give bird **black-capped look**. Wings narrower, more pointed than other alcids in Region.

Similar Species: Ancient Murrelet (see inset; breeds British Columbia, Alaska, Siberia, small numbers present in Region late fall–early winter). Same size as Marbled, with **yellow bill, gray back, no white streak** where wings join back. Black chin, nape, crown, less-extensive white collar give bird **white-cheeked look. Underwing white** (dark in Marbled).

Seasonal Abundance: Uncommon year-round resident in Region; in winter usually seen in pairs. Ranges Aleutians to California; populations seriously declining.

Where to Find: Relatively shallow saltwater bays, inlets, passages, especially northern part of Region (Admiralty Inlet, Rosario Strait, San Juan Islands). Ancient Murrelet similarly distributed.

Habitat: Nests in forests away from coast, commuting to salt water to forage; winters on protected marine waters.

Diet and Behavior: Dives for small fish, crustaceans, other sea animals. Flies with rapid wingbeats.

Voice: Flight call loud, high-pitched *keer keer keer* series, mostly near nest.

Did you know? The first Marbled Murrelet nest was discovered only in 1974.

Date & Location Seen: _____

Breeding

Description: 15", wingspan 22". Head, wings, body above water line **dark-gray-brown**; light belly visible in flight. **Large yellow bill** (gray in juveniles). BREEDING: **White plumes** form streaks behind eye, bill; variable short "horn" at base of upper bill.

Similar Species: Marbled Murrelet (page 183) in breeding plumage much smaller, thin-billed, with darker belly. Tufted Puffin (not shown; a few nest on Protection Island) similar in coloration in juvenal plumage, but much heavier with huge bill; dark belly visible in flight.

Seasonal Abundance: Common resident in Region, April–September; uncommon winter resident. Breeds on Protection, Smith Islands; majority winter at sea. Ranges along both sides of Pacific from Aleutians south to Japan, California.

Where to Find: April–September, eastern Strait of Juan de Fuca, e.g., Port Townsend–Coupeville ferry, Washington Park (Anacortes), Deception Pass State Park, San Juan Islands ferry. In winter, most numerous in South Sound, e.g., Point Defiance Park (Tacoma).

Habitat: Salt water, usually fairly deep (60 feet or more). Often forages in tide rips.

Diet and Behavior: Dives for fish. Nests colonially, visiting nests only at night.

Voice: Mostly silent away from nests.

Did you know? Male and female "Rhinos" excavate nest burrows up to 15 feet deep in soil on grassy, brushy slopes well above the shoreline.

Date & Location Seen: _____

Description: 13″, wingspan 28″. Familiar domestic pigeon, **highly variable in color, patterning**. Most common form gray with **dark bill**, flesh-colored legs, dark head, neck; iridescent feathers on neck, two black bars across wing, **black band at tip of tail. White rump, underwing** visible in flight.

Similar Species: Band-tailed Pigeon (page 189) has yellow bill with black tip; gray, not white rump, white on nape of neck, broad gray band on tail, yellow legs, dark underwing.

Seasonal Abundance: Common, widespread year-round resident in Region. Native to Old World; domesticated birds introduced, now naturalized essentially worldwide.

Where to Find: City parks, streets, industrial zones; bridges, overpasses; rural seed fields, barns, grain elevators.

Habitat: Lowlands. Cities, towns, rural settings near human habitation.

Diet and Behavior: Forages mostly on ground for grain, seeds, grasses, food scraps. Feeds, travels in flocks. Flies at speeds up to 85 miles per hour – one of fastest birds in Region.

Voice: Soft cooing.

Did you know? Introduced by early European settlers, the Rock Pigeon is now widespread throughout North America and one of the most abundant urban birds, building nests on window ledges, water towers, bridges, and other structures.

Date & Location Seen: _____

BAND-TAILED PIGEON
Patagioenas fasciata

Description: 14″, wingspan 26″. Overall gray with purplish head, breast, **black-tipped yellow bill, gray rump, pale-gray band on tail, yellow legs**, white bar above iridescent feathers on nape (absent in juveniles). **Dark underwing** visible in flight.

Similar Species: Rock Pigeon (page 187) has white, not gray, rump, flesh-colored legs, all-dark bill, white underwing.

Seasonal Abundance: Fairly common summer resident in Region, uncommon in winter; most go south September–October, return beginning late February. Ranges from southwestern British Columbia, Colorado, to Argentina.

Where to Find: Well-treed neighborhoods, parks, marine shorelines, foothills, e.g., Larrabee State Park, Rockport State Park, Rattlesnake Lake Recreation Area.

Habitat: Breeds low-elevation coniferous, mixed forests; uncommon to mountain passes. Prefers tall conifers, forest edges with nearby open spaces. Post-breeders, migrants regular in mountains.

Diet and Behavior: Feeds mostly on nuts, seeds, fruits of deciduous trees, shrubs such as oak, cherry, elderberry, madrone, cascara. Attracted to feeders with black-oil sunflower, cracked corn, millet. Usually forages, travels in small flocks. When taking flight, wings produce loud clapping noise.

Voice: Low, repetitive *whoo oo whoo*.

Did you know? Band-tailed Pigeons make morning visits to mineral springs with nearby roosting trees, especially in summer – for example, Nisqually National Wildlife Refuge, Mud Bay (Thurston County), Sumas Springs (Whatcom County).

Date & Location Seen: _____

Eurasian Collared-Dove

Mourning Dove

Description: 12" / 11", wingspan 22" / 18". COLLARED: **Bulky; pale** grayish-brown with **blunt-tipped tail, black collar** on nape, **gray undertail**. MOURNING: **Slender**; mostly **tan-colored** with **long, pointed tail**, black spots on wings; male has pinkish hue to breast, bluish crown.

Similar Species: African Collared-Dove (not shown; also called Ringed Turtle-Dove) similar to Eurasian but smaller, much paler, with white undertail; occurs as escaped cage bird.

Seasonal Abundance: COLLARED: Uncommon but increasing resident in Region. Native to Eurasia; introduced to North America. MOURNING: Uncommon, local resident in Region; many migrate south for winter. Ranges from southern Canada to Middle America.

Where to Find: Throughout lowlands. Shun dense forest, urban core.

Habitat: Grasslands (prairie, agricultural), farms, grain elevators, small woodlots, semi-rural residential tracts, towns.

Diet and Behavior: Diet almost exclusively seeds taken on ground, sometimes feeders. Often seen on overhead wires. Form flocks, especially in winter, at sites with plentiful food, nearby trees for sheltering, roosting.

Voice: COLLARED: "Song" *coo coo coop* (stress on second syllable). MOURNING: Slow, mournful *ooo aaa ooo ooo ooo*.

Did you know? Introduced to the New World in the Bahamas in 1972, Eurasian Collared-Doves reached Washington in 30 years.

Date & Location Seen: _____

Description: 15", wingspan 40". **Slim, long-legged, round-headed owl** with prominent **heart-shaped facial disc**, dark-brown eyes, long, yellowish, hooked bill. Brownish-tan back with pearl-gray spots, mostly white underparts impart **pale appearance**. In flight, tail looks fairly long, wings appear bowed.

Similar Species: Barred Owl (page 201) bulkier, broader-winged. Short-eared Owl (page 203) has floppier flight, dark wing patches.

Seasonal Abundance: Fairly common resident in Region. Ranges worldwide in temperate, tropical zones.

Where to Find: Lowlands, including cities.

Habitat: Open areas: farmland, fields, wetlands, clearcuts, urban landscapes with buildings, trees for day roosting.

Diet and Behavior: Extremely nocturnal. Hunts from perches or in low flight by sight, sound, captures prey in talons. Directional hearing well-developed for locating rodents, its primary quarry, in high grass. Also takes some birds, insects, cold-blooded animals. Roosts in buildings or dense conifers by day. Does not build nest; lays up to 10 eggs in dark corner of building, large nest box, cave, tree cavity.

Voice: Varied calls include harsh, grating screech, long hiss, series of metallic clicks.

Did you know? One Barn Owl can eat over 1,500 mice per year.

Date & Location Seen: _____

Description: 7½". **Small** but robust, mottled grayish or brownish, **block-headed** with **prominent ear tufts** (sometimes held flat), **yellow eyes**. Breast, belly streaked, finely barred.

Similar Species: Combination of small size, ear tufts, yellow eyes eliminates other owls.

Seasonal Abundance: Fairly common resident in Region. Ranges across West, southeastern Alaska–Mexico.

Where to Find: Local; often absent in suitable-looking habitat. Mostly lowlands, river drainages up to moderate elevation. Good areas include West Seattle parks, eastern King County woodlands.

Habitat: Broadleaf, mixed woodlands, including forest edge, parks, backyards. Often along watercourses.

Diet and Behavior: Extremely nocturnal. Hunts from perches, swoops, captures prey in talons. Locates prey by sight, sound. Favors rodents, large insects, but will take birds, reptiles, amphibians. Does not build nest; uses existing tree cavities. Usually responds to imitations of its calls by approaching, calling to protect territory.

Voice: Common call accelerating series of low whistles in pattern of ball bouncing, then coming to rest (notes start far apart, higher, get progressively closer together, lower).

Did you know? Distributed throughout the New World, the more than 20 small, tufted owls of the genus *Megascops* are often closely similar. Researchers only recently concluded that Western and Eastern Screech-Owls were two separate species, based on differences in vocalizations.

Date & Location Seen: _____

GREAT HORNED OWL
Bubo virginianus

Description: 22", wingspan 45". Formidable owl, mottled grayish-brown, **block-headed** with **prominent ear tufts. Yellow eyes,** brownish facial disc, **white throat**, finely-barred lower breast, belly.

Similar Species: Long-eared Owl (not shown; rare in Region) also has prominent ear tufts, but smaller (15", one-fifth as heavy) with vertical streaks below.

Seasonal Abundance: Fairly common resident in countryside in Region, somewhat less common in cities (may increase with influx of fall transients). Ranges throughout New World, from Arctic to South America.

Where to Find: Lowlands to tree line, although uncommon in dense conifer forest.

Habitat: Adaptable. Woodlands, meadows, farmlands, city parks.

Diet and Behavior: Hunts mostly at night, watching, listening for prey from perch, then pursuing, capturing it with talons. Diet extremely varied, mostly small mammals but also birds, large insects, cold-blooded animals including fish. Does not build nest; uses snags, cavities, nests of other species, especially Red-tailed Hawk. One of earliest nesting birds, lays eggs as early as January.

Voice: Common call deep *whoo whodoo whoo who*. Begging young give harsh shrieks.

Did you know? Great Horned Owls are powerful, fearless hunters. They have been recorded killing and eating animals as large as Great Blue Herons and skunks.

Date & Location Seen: _____

Description: 22", wingspan 50". **Round-headed, yellow-eyed, mostly white**, varying amounts of dark mottling. Adult male may be pure white; female, immature may have dense, dark barring.

Similar Species: None in Region.

Seasonal Abundance: Not present in Region most years. Periodically irrupts southward (November–early April) due to high reproduction, subsequent food shortage in Arctic where nests, normally winters. Numbers in Region at such times usually only 1–2; can reach 12 or more at favored sites. Ranges around northern hemisphere in tundra belt.

Where to Find: When present, concentrates in open coastal habitats. Appears anywhere food present, including cities. Best bets Skagit, Samish, Lummi Flats, Dungeness Spit.

Habitat: Agricultural fields, beaches, intertidal zone, salt marshes, estuaries, urban areas.

Diet and Behavior: Hunts mostly at dusk, dawn but takes prey any time. Sits on ground, other low perches, structures; takes flight, captures prey with talons. Prefers small mammals, but takes larger animals including waterfowl, other owls. Often concentrates in loose groups near flocks of waterfowl (important food source in Region).

Voice: Almost entirely silent in winter. Screams, hoots on tundra.

Did you know? Snowy Owls' long, pointed wings – an adaptation for rapid flight to catch prey in the open – give them the appearance of a large-headed falcon in flight.

Date & Location Seen: _____

Description: 19", wingspan 42". Bulky, grayish, with **dark-brown eyes. Rounded head** with white lines in ring-like pattern above dark-bordered facial disc. Hooked bill yellowish, upperparts mottled, streaked. **Upper breast barred; lower breast, belly whitish with dark streaks**.

Similar Species: Great Horned Owl (page 197) has ear tufts, yellow eyes. Barn Owl (page 193) slimmer. Spotted Owl (not shown; rare resident of old-growth forests in Region) dark-brown, lacks streaks below.

Seasonal Abundance: Recent arrival in Region, now fairly common resident. Ranges throughout eastern U.S., across southern Canada to Northwest.

Where to Find: Throughout Region including parks within cites.

Habitat: Wet mixed, broadleaf forests; prefers dense woods but may disperse in fall to more urbanized settings.

Diet and Behavior: Mostly nocturnal. Hunts from perches; favors rodents, but eats other small mammals, birds, reptiles, amphibians, large insects. Does not build nest – uses large cavities, nests of other species. Vocal, territorial, occasionally even toward humans.

Voice: Loud hoots including *who cooks for you, who cooks for you allll* sequence.

Did you know? Barred Owls first reached Washington in 1965, in the far northeastern corner of the state. Due to logging-related alteration of forest habitats they have now supplanted the closely-related Spotted Owl in most of the Region.

Date & Location Seen: _____

Description: 14″, wingspan 38″. **Moth-like flight** on long, broad wings. Streaked upperparts, upper breast, light below. In flight shows **dark patch near wrist**, buff patch toward outer end of upperwing. Yellow eyes, prominent facial disc; short ear tufts seldom visible.

Similar Species: Slow, floppy flight, daytime activity unlike other large owls in Region.

Seasonal Abundance: Fairly common migrant, winter resident in Region (October–April); once regular breeder but few recent records. Ranges through much of northern hemisphere, vacating northern parts in winter; also resident in South America.

Where to Find: Quite local in open habitat. Most common Skagit, Whatcom Counties. Best bets Skagit, Samish Flats.

Habitat: Open, wet meadows, fallow agricultural fields, coastal marshes.

Diet and Behavior: Highly migratory, nomadic. Hunts low over fields, mostly near dawn, dusk, but may fly at night and in full daylight. Locates voles, other small mammals, birds by sight, sound, often hovering before pouncing, capturing with talons. Concentrates in loose flocks at areas of prey abundance, roosts on ground by day.

Voice: Gives nasal barks, wheezy whistles when multiple birds hunt.

Did you know? Short-eared Owls nest on the ground. As many as ten young may leave a nest in as little as two weeks.

Date & Location Seen: _____

Juvenile

Description: 7″. Small, **round-headed, yellow-eyed** owl, white below with broad, brown streaking, brown back, large white wing spots, **fine white streaks on face, head**. JUVENILE: Plain-brown, ochre below, with white forehead.

Similar Species: Western Screech-Owl (page 195) larger, block-headed, with ear tufts (although these may be held flat). Northern Pygmy-Owl (not shown; uncommon in Region) smaller, with long tail, smaller head, typically active in daylight. Boreal Owl (not shown; limited to high mountains) rather similar but larger.

Seasonal Abundance: Fairly common resident in Region but seldom seen, numbers augmented in winter by migrants. Ranges across North America from southeastern Alaska to eastern Maritimes, south in mountains to Mexico.

Where to Find: Sea level to mountain passes; scarce in urban areas.

Habitat: Coniferous, mixed woodlands, often near water.

Diet and Behavior: Extremely nocturnal. Locates prey by sight, sound; favors rodents, also takes birds, insects. Nests in tree cavities, habitually roosts in one spot in dense conifers where best located by resulting pile of feces. Strongly migratory; may move south or downslope in fall.

Voice: Calls including rhythmic tooting, *skews*, twitters, barks, whining whistles, may be elicited by imitation of its tooting call.

Did you know? Emaciated Northern Saw-whet Owls may appear near bird feeders in winter.

Date & Location Seen: _____

Description: 9½", wingspan 24". Short-legged, relatively long-tailed, **mottled grayish-brown** above, banded brown below; **long, pointed, angular wings with conspicuous broad white band** near tip. **Usually seen high in flight.** Appears owl-like at rest; wingtips extend beyond tail tip. MALE: White chin, tail band. FEMALE: Buffy chin.

Similar Species: Swallows, swifts much smaller; falcons have more direct flight, lack white wing bands.

Seasonal Abundance: Uncommon migrant, summer resident in Region (late May–early September). Highly migratory; breeds across most of North, Middle America, winters South America.

Where to Find: Sparse breeder in mountains, rural lowlands (San Juan, Kitsap, Mason Counties, South Sound Prairies). Late-summer transients seen regularly in metropolitan areas of southern part of Region.

Habitat: Open habitats: forest clearings, stony ground, weedy lots. Hunts, migrates over cities, forests, fields.

Diet and Behavior: Forages aerially with erratic flight – mostly near dawn, dusk, but active at any hour. Short bill opens to huge gape for catching insects. Perches lengthwise along branches. Nests on open ground, relying on camouflage. In courtship males dive steeply, producing booming sound.

Voice: Far-carrying nasal buzz given repeatedly in flight.

Did you know? Nighthawks belong to a group of birds called goatsuckers, which are most closely related to owls. Two other nighthawk species reach the southern United States.

Date & Location Seen: _____

_____

Black Swift

Vaux's Swift

Description: BLACK largest North American swift (7¼", 1.6 oz.), VAUX'S smallest (4¾", 0.7 oz.). Both darkish overall, usually seen foraging high overhead on **pointed, curving wings** with **flickering wing-beats**. BLACK: **Broader wingbase, longer tail (often notched). Wing-beat slower, shallower; glides frequently.** VAUX'S: **Throat, breast, rump paler** than rest of plumage (hard to spot in field); short tail tapers to point when closed, giving **"winged cigar"** look. **Wing-beat rapid** with only brief intervals of gliding.

Similar Species: Swallows may use similar aerial foraging strategy, but wing-beats not so flickering; wings proportionally shorter, broader, less swept-back.

Seasonal Abundance: Summer residents in Region, locally fairly common. Return May, depart August–September. Main nesting ranges southeastern Alaska to Central America; winter from Mexico to South America.

Where to Find: Darrington, Index, Snoqualmie Valley, Lake Washington, Spencer Island, Mount Rainier, many other sites.

Habitat: BLACK: Nests North Cascades, forages in lowlands when clouds envelop mountains. VAUX'S: Nests widely in hollow trees (occasionally chimneys). Both hunt opportunistically, often over wetlands, lakes, streams.

Diet and Behavior: Small insects taken on wing.

Voice: Chip notes. BLACK often in series; VAUX'S rapid, higher-pitched.

Did you know? Washington's first Black Swift nest was found in 2012 in Whatcom County. Vaux's Swifts roost communally in smokestacks, belfries, hollow trees in fall migration.

Date & Location Seen: _____

_____

Male

Female

Description: 4". MALE: Green back, grayish underparts, **iridescent-red crown**, throat (can appear black in shadow), dark tail. FEMALE: Similar except outer tail feathers tipped white, red restricted to small spot on throat. IMMATURE: Little or no red.

Similar Species: Female/immature Rufous Hummingbirds (page 213) have rufous flanks, tail base, undertail.

Seasonal Abundance: Common year-round resident in Region; increasing, spreading. Original range along Pacific Coast from northern Baja California to San Francisco Bay; now breeds north to Vancouver Island, east to Arizona.

Where to Find: Lowlands, especially cities, towns. Reliable at Discovery Park (Seattle).

Habitat: Human-influenced: parks, gardens, residential neighborhoods. Hummingbird feeders, exotic flowering plants may help account for phenomenally successful range extension.

Diet and Behavior: Consumes nectar from flowers, sugar-water from hummingbird feeders, sap from holes in trees (often drilled by sapsuckers), small insects, spiders. Can survive short bouts of severe cold weather by lowering body temperature at night, converting more sugar to fat, or entering torpor (dormancy).

Voice: Loud chip note. Song dry, rasping, delivered year round from exposed perch. Various squeaks, buzzes, chattering sounds in courtship, territorial defense.

Did you know? Male Anna's defend their territories with "dive displays", looping 60–120 feet into the air then zooming down to emit a loud pop in the intruder's face.

Date & Location Seen: _____

Male

Female

Description: 3³/₄". Bill straight, dark. MALE: **Back, tail, underparts rusty-orange**; back may have variable amounts of green. Crown green, upper breast white, throat iridescent orange-red. FEMALE: Upperparts, crown green; **tail base, undertail, flanks rufous**; outer tail feathers white-tipped. Red feathering on throat varies from none up to small spot. IMMATURE: Resembles female.

Similar Species: Female/immature Anna's Hummingbirds (page 211) show no rufous coloration.

Seasonal Abundance: Common summer resident in Region. Breeds from northern California to western Montana, southern Alaska; winters in southern U.S., Mexico. Males arrive before females in spring, sometimes by late February.

Where to Find: Widespread (e.g., Nisqually National Wildlife Refuge, Lake Sammamish State Park, Skagit Wildlife Area). North Cascades Highway, houses with feeders at Snoqualmie Pass sure bets in summer.

Habitat: Forest openings, disturbed areas, brushy edges; lowlands in spring, moves up into flowering meadows in mountains as season progresses.

Diet and Behavior: Consumes nectar from flowers, sugar-water from hummingbird feeders, sap from holes in trees, small insects, spiders. Male has diving courtship display.

Voice: Chip, other warning notes. No song. Adult male's wings make high-pitched whine.

Did you know? Rufous Hummingbird is the northernmost representative of this largely tropical New World family. It is also the smallest bird in the Puget Sound Region.

Date & Location Seen: _____

Male

Female

Description: 13". **Large head, unkempt crest, stout bill**. MALE: Mostly **slate-blue with white underparts, collar; wide slate-blue breastband**. FEMALE: Identical but with rufous flanks, additional rufous band across lower breast. JUVENILE: Single dark breast band, rufous flanks.

Similar Species: None in Region.

Seasonal Abundance: Common year-round resident in Region. Nests continent wide – below Arctic tundra, north of arid Southwest. Retreats from northernmost parts at freezeup; winters along Pacific Coast (Aleutians south), across most of U.S., throughout Mexico, Caribbean (a few farther south).

Where to Find: From sea level to tree line, any stretch of shore with good nest sites, fishing prospects has its pair of kingfishers.

Habitat: Along streams, lakes, ponds, saltwater shorelines with clear, relatively still waters where it can see prey.

Diet and Behavior: Watches from perch over water, or hovers; plunges in shallow dive (less than two feet below surface), seizes prey in bill. Takes mostly fish, some insects, crustaceans, other animals. Digs nest burrows, usually 3–6 feet deep in banks.

Voice: Main call loud rattle, somewhat like sound of ratchet noisemaker toy, given all year (often in flight).

Did you know? A Belted Kingfisher returns to its perch with a freshly caught fish in its bill, beats it senseless against the perch, then swallows it headfirst.

Date & Location Seen: _____

Juvenile

RED-BREASTED SAPSUCKER
Sphyrapicus ruber

Description: 8½". Typical woodpecker tree-clinging behavior, undulating flight, chisel-like bill. Colorful. Breast, **head entirely red** except for faint white mustache mark; belly yellowish, back black with white mottling. Elongated **white patch across center of upperwing**. JUVENILE: Dark-brownish, molts to adult plumage by September.

Similar Species: Red-naped Sapsucker (not shown; rare in Region except at Cascade crest) has white facial lines, no red below throat. Much larger Pileated Woodpecker (page 225) crested, with small white patch closer to end of wing.

Seasonal Abundance: Fairly common resident in Region. Ranges down coast, southeastern Alaska to Baja California.

Where to Find: Coniferous, mixed forests; in winter may use urban parks, backyards, small woodlots.

Habitat: Prefers cedar-hemlock-spruce-dominated forests, but also found in various mixed woods.

Diet and Behavior: Quietly drills evenly-spaced small holes in live trees, revisiting these "wells" on regular foraging routes to drink sap, feed on insects attracted to sap, berries, tree tissues. Moves downslope below level of heavy snow in winter. Excavates nest hole in conifer snag, aspen, or other soft wood.

Voice: Calls include nasal mews, squeals; territorial drumming irregularly spaced.

Did you know? Red-breasted Sapsucker interbreeds with the closely-related Red-naped Sapsucker at the Cascade crest, resulting in intermediate-plumaged hybrids.

Date & Location Seen: _____

Male   Female

Description: 6¾". **Short, chisel-like bill**, stiff tail, tree-clinging behavior. **Dingy-white or buffy back**, underparts, eyebrow, mustache mark; black bars on white outer tail feathers; **wings checkered black-and-white**. MALE: Red spot at back of head. JUVENILE: Red on top of head.

Similar Species: Hairy Woodpecker (page 221) identical but larger, with bill as long as distance from back of head to bill base (Downy's bill only half this measurement).

Seasonal Abundance: Common lowland resident in Region, becoming uncommon at higher elevations. Ranges from Alaska to Labrador, south to Florida, Texas, California.

Where to Find: Woodlands, parks, neighborhoods, stream corridors, semi-open rural habitats, mostly at low elevations.

Habitat: Prefers broadleaf woods, but also found in mixed forests, hedgerows, thickets.

Diet and Behavior: Probes dead limbs, small twigs, weed stalks in search of insects, also feeds on fruits, seeds. Excavates nest cavity in dead wood; calls, drums to establish territory. Common at suet feeders. Flight undulating, like that of other woodpeckers.

Voice: Calls include rattle-like whinny, flat *pik* (not as sharp as that given by Hairy Woodpecker).

Did you know? Male and female Downy Woodpeckers often maintain separate feeding territories in winter.

Date & Location Seen: _____

Male Female

Description: 9½″. **Long chisel-like bill**, stiff tail, tree-clinging behavior. **Dingy-white back**, underparts, eyebrow, mustache mark, outer tail feathers; **wings checkered black-and-white**. MALE: Red spot at back of head. JUVENILE: Red on top of head.

Similar Species: Downy Woodpecker (page 219) identical but smaller, shorter-billed, with black spots on outer tail (juvenile Hairy may also show these).

Seasonal Abundance: Fairly common resident in Region. Ranges from Alaska to Labrador, south to Central America, Caribbean.

Where to Find: Throughout Region although scarce in urban areas.

Habitat: Prefers coniferous forest, but also uses mixed, broadleaf woods.

Diet and Behavior: Excavates dead wood, scrapes bark, probes in search of insects; may also feed on fruits, seeds, sap. Digs nest cavities in live or dead wood; drums, calls to establish territory. Regular at bird feeders. Flight undulating, like that of other woodpeckers.

Voice: Calls include *pik krrreeeeer*, very sharp *piik* (louder than similar call given by Downy Woodpecker).

Did you know? Hairy Woodpeckers resident west of the Cascades are dingy-white. In winter, small numbers of bright-white birds descend from the mountains to western Washington lowlands.

Date & Location Seen: _____

Red-shafted
Male

Yellow-shafted
Male

Red-shafted
Female

Description: 12". Robust, colorful, with **black crescent bib, white rump**. Long bill, stiff tail, tree-clinging behavior. Barred brown above, spotted buff below, with **brightly-colored feather shafts**, most notable in wings. Two forms. RED-SHAFTED: Brown cap, gray face, **red shafts**, male with red mustache mark. YELLOW-SHAFTED: Gray cap, brown face, **yellow shafts, red crescent on nape**, male with black mustache mark.

Similar Species: Distinctive in Region.

Seasonal Abundance: Common resident in Region but highly migratory. Ranges throughout North America, Central America, Caribbean. Yellow-shafted, Red-shafted forms interbreed where ranges overlap along eastern slope of Rocky Mountains.

Where to Find: Throughout Region.

Habitat: Open woodlands, any semi-open area, urban woodlots, lawns.

Diet and Behavior: Forages on ground for ants, in trees for fruits, occasionally seeds where available. Loud calling, drumming, boisterous interactions, ability to thrive in urban areas make it noticeable. Excavates cavity nest in live or dead wood. Flight undulating, like that of other woodpeckers. Flocks in migration.

Voice: Calls include *woika woika woika*, long series of repeated *kuk* notes, piercing *keeww*.

Did you know? The red-shafted form resides year round in the Region. Yellow-shafted birds are present fall to spring along with intergrades that show mixed characteristics.

Date & Location Seen: _____

Male

PILEATED WOODPECKER
Dryocopus pileatus

Description: 16". Chisel-like bill, stiff tail, tree-clinging behavior, undulating flight typical of woodpeckers. **Large**, lanky; **black** except for **large crimson crest, white neck stripe**, facial markings, underwings, wing patch. MALE: Red mustache mark.

Similar Species: Much larger than other woodpeckers in Region. Red, white markings, undulating flight distinguish it from crows.

Seasonal Abundance: Fairly common resident in Region. Ranges across southern Canada, U.S., except for most of interior West.

Where to Find: Throughout Region, including forest tracts, parks within urban areas.

Habitat: Mature coniferous, mixed forests.

Diet and Behavior: Excavates large, deep, oval or rectangular holes in trees in search of insects, primarily ants. Chisels through hard wood to access insect-damaged tree centers. Also feeds on small fruits. Sometimes loud, obvious with tapping, banging, calling, but also secretive, hiding behind tree trunks. Often calls while flying above or within canopy.

Voice: Series of 10–15 wild-sounding *kuk* notes with irregular rhythm, abrupt ending. Territorial drumming slow, loud.

Did you know? With the extinction of the Ivory-billed Woodpecker of the southeastern United States and Cuba and the Imperial Woodpecker of Mexico, the Pileated Woodpecker is now the largest member of the woodpecker family on the North American continent.

Date & Location Seen: _____

Male

Female

Description: 10", wingspan 21". **Delicate**, long-tailed falcon with **russet back**, gray-and-rufous crown, **two black stripes on white face**. MALE: Long, **pointed wings**, blue-gray above, solid-russet tail ending in wide black band, narrow white tip. Breast rusty in adult, streaked in immature. FEMALE: Similar; wings, tail russet with fine banding, breast streaked.

Similar Species: Merlin (page 127) chunkier; darkly streaked below with broadly-banded tail, vague mustache mark, more powerful flight.

Seasonal Abundance: Uncommon resident in Region, numbers augmented by migrants. Ranges across North America south of tree line, winters as far south as Central America.

Where to Find: Sparsely distributed year round in lowlands, also mountains in summer. Good locations include Hurricane Ridge, Samish Flats.

Habitat: Open areas such as farmland, alpine meadows, forest edges, clearings.

Diet and Behavior: Hunts for insects, small mammals, small birds from perches or by stationary hovering over field. Nests in natural cavities (usually trees) but also uses nest boxes. Defends territory by calling, flying at intruders.

Voice: Common call series of piercing *kli* notes.

Did you know? American Kestrels are highly migratory. Winter residents in the Puget Sound Region may be migrants from farther north, while summer residents may go south.

Date & Location Seen: _____

Description: 11″, wingspan 23″. Compact, **swift-flying**, small falcon. Plumage varies with race, but generally **heavily streaked below** with plain, dark back, **banded tail, vague mustache mark**. Appears dark in flight with **sharply-pointed wings**. MALE: Adult with gray back, cap. FEMALE: Larger, browner. JUVENILE: Brown.

Similar Species: Peregrine Falcon (page 129) larger with prominent mustache mark. American Kestrel (page 125) lighter below, finely built, with distinct head markings.

Seasonal Abundance: Fairly common but easily-overlooked migrant, winter resident in Region; rare breeder. Ranges across northern forests of Eurasia, North America, winters to southern tropics.

Where to Find: Mostly lowlands. Easiest to find in cities, towns, or near coastal concentrations of Dunlins.

Habitat: Coastal marshes, agricultural flats, broken woodlands, urban areas.

Diet and Behavior: Makes dashing flights from perch, captures prey with talons at blinding speed. Diet almost exclusively small songbirds, shorebirds. Rarely soars; typical flight observation bullet-like pass. More likely spotted perched atop prominent snags, conifers. Aggressively harasses other raptors many times its size.

Voice: Rarely vocal away from nest; calls include series of *twi* notes.

Did you know? Merlins are extremely rare breeders in the Olympics and the Cascades. Nesting reports from the lowlands of the Puget Sound Region, including cities in the northern part, are increasing.

Date & Location Seen: _____

Immature

Description: 16", wingspan 43". Sleek, powerfully built, **crow-sized** falcon with **thick mustache mark**, long **wings reaching tail tip when perched**. Gray above, dark barring below, variable salmon-colored or whitish bib. **Sharply pointed wings** in flight. IMMATURE: Browner with streaking instead of barring; bill, skin around eye pale-blue (yellow in adult).

Similar Species: Merlin (page 127) smaller, mustache mark less distinct. Two other falcons rare in Region (not shown). Prairie Falcon browner with dark armpits; Gyrfalcon bulkier with shorter, broader wings.

Seasonal Abundance: Uncommon resident in Region, numbers augmented by migrants, wintering birds late September–May. Many races range worldwide.

Where to Find: Most common in lowlands; nests in Cascade foothills, San Juan Islands, cities. Good bets include Samish Flats, other wintering shorebird, waterfowl sites.

Habitat: Seacoasts, cities, agricultural fields, tidal flats. Requires cliffs, buildings, other tall structures for nesting, often near water.

Diet and Behavior: Catches live birds in mid-air, making spectacular dives at speeds up to 200 miles per hour. Prey ranges from songbirds to ducks; Rock Pigeons, shorebirds favored. Rarely eats mammals, carrion. Nests on bare ledge, fiercely defends territory.

Voice: Calls include harsh, piercing series of *keh* notes.

Did you know? Peregrine Falcons were taken off the Endangered Species List in 1999 after numbers rebounded from pesticide-caused declines.

Date & Location Seen: _____

OLIVE-SIDED FLYCATCHER
Contopus cooperi

Description: 7½". **Upright stance**, dark grayish-olive above, below, with wide white line extending from throat down chest to belly giving **vested appearance. Large head** with slight crest, long, dark bill, **short tail**, impart stout profile. White rump tufts seldom visible.

Similar Species: Western Wood-Pewee (page 235) smaller, appears less vested, with smaller bill.

Seasonal Abundance: Fairly common May–September resident in Region, with migration, dispersal continuing throughout summer. Breeds from Alaska to Labrador, south in western mountains to New Mexico; winters to South America.

Where to Find: Throughout Region. Declining as breeder within urban areas.

Habitat: Fairly mature coniferous forest; prefers tree stands interspersed with open areas, including clearcuts, old burns, bogs, neighborhoods, parks.

Diet and Behavior: Makes wide-ranging sallies for large flying insects from exposed perch at top of tree or snag. Usually returns to perch in same spot. Calls frequently; best located by voice.

Voice: Song whistled *quick three beers* with second syllable strongly accented. Calls include *pep pep pep* repeated at short intervals.

Did you know? The Olive-sided Flycatcher is declining in numbers, especially in the East. Suggested causes include tropical habitat loss and a reduction in prey availability.

Date & Location Seen: _____

Description: 6". **Upright stance**, dark-olive-gray above, long wings with light-colored **wing-bars, dusky chest**, pale-yellowish belly. Slim with **fairly prominent crest**, dark bill with lighter base, **no eye-ring**.

Similar Species: More crested, but easily confused with smaller, lighter *Empidonax* flycatchers (pages 237–241). Olive-side Flycatcher (page 233) larger with shorter tail, larger head, more vested appearance.

Seasonal Abundance: Fairly common resident in Region from mid-May to mid-September. Breeds in West from Alaska south in mountains to Honduras, winters in South America.

Where to Find: Mostly lowlands but occurs to mountain passes. Seldom nests within urban areas but widespread in migration.

Habitat: Open woodlands, woodland edge, preferring broadleaf growth along water courses.

Diet and Behavior: Forages from exposed perch in tall shrub or tree, making sallies to capture insects; may return to same spot. Often flutters wings while perching. Calls throughout day in spring, early summer, so best located by voice.

Voice: Most frequent call burry, nasal *prreeer*. Song, given at dawn, combination of tones similar to call.

Did you know? Western Wood-Pewees build their nests on the horizontal surface of limbs, usually at a fork.

Date & Location Seen: _____

Description: 5½". Fairly distinctive member of look-alike *Empidonax* flycatcher group. **Upright stance**; olive-brown above, buff-white wing-bars, whitish underparts. **Appears slim**, fairly long, with **long, broad, pale bill. Eye-ring minimal or absent**.

Similar Species: Other *Empidonax* flycatchers in Region have prominent eye-rings. Western Wood-Pewee (page 235) slightly larger, much darker overall with more crested appearance.

Seasonal Abundance: Common resident in Region mid-May to September. Ranges across continent from extreme southern Canada south to California, Georgia; winters from Mexico to Panama.

Where to Find: Mostly at lower elevation, but also up to mountain passes in clearcuts. Nests within urban areas in appropriate habitat, scarce in migration away from nesting locations.

Habitat: Open, shrubby, wetland habitats, clearcuts, brushy forest edge.

Diet and Behavior: Forages from perch usually within tall shrub, making sallies to capture insects. Eats some berries in summer, fall. Easily located by voice: distinctive song given throughout day, but especially near dawn.

Voice: Harsh *fitz bew* song, with first syllable strongly accented. Calls include clear *whit*, buzzy *breet*.

Did you know? Identification of *Empidonax* flycatchers is notoriously difficult. The Alder Flycatcher – a close relative of the Willow Flycatcher that breeds farther north – is so similar that the two can be told apart only by their vocalizations.

Date & Location Seen: _____

Description: 5". Difficult-to-identify member of look-alike *Empidonax* flycatcher group. **Upright stance; appears dark, large-headed**, long-winged. Grayish-green with wing-bars, yellowish wash on belly, **dusky-gray chest**, gray head with distinct eye-ring. Short bill may appear all-dark.

Similar Species: Pacific-slope Flycatcher (page 241) slimmer, brighter, with more asymmetrical eye-ring. Willow Flycatcher (page 237) without eye-ring. Other *Empidonax* species rare in Region (not shown). Western Wood-Pewee (page 235) larger, no eye-ring.

Seasonal Abundance: Fairly common resident in Region, mid-April to September. Breeds in West, Alaska to New Mexico; winters in highlands from southeastern Arizona to Honduras.

Where to Find: Nests in older coniferous forests throughout Region, away from urban areas. Scarce on islands, near coast; most easily found from middle elevations to mountain passes. Widespread in migration.

Habitat: Prefers dense coniferous forests but also uses mixed woods, broadleaf thickets in migration.

Diet and Behavior: Forages from perch, making sallies to capture insect prey. Often flicks tail, wings nervously. Feeds at all levels, but often remains high in dense conifer growth.

Voice: Song consists of several phrases including burry, distinctive *bureek*. Calls include sharp *peet*.

Did you know? Hammond's Flycatchers can appear brightly colored in fall – they molt into fresh plumage before migrating.

Date & Location Seen: _____

PACIFIC-SLOPE FLYCATCHER
Empidonax difficilis

Description: 5¼". Fairly distinctive member of look-alike *Empidonax* flycatcher group. **Upright stance**; olive-green with wing-bars; yellow wash on underparts extends up to throat. Wide, **pale bill, slightly crested appearance**; strong, **asymmetrical eye-ring**, elongated behind eye.

Similar Species: Other *Empidonax* flycatchers in Region less yellow on upper breast, throat, with less prominent, more symmetrical eye-ring. Smaller, lighter-colored than Western Wood-Pewee (page 235).

Seasonal Abundance: Common resident in Region, mid-April to September. Breeds from southeastern Alaska south through Pacific states to Baja California, winters in Mexico.

Where to Find: Nests throughout Region from lowlands to mountain passes, including smaller wooded tracts within urban areas. Migrants also use thickets in parks, neighborhoods.

Habitat: Shaded interior of moist, mixed or coniferous forests, preferably with broadleaf understory.

Diet and Behavior: Forages by watching for insects while perched within leafy growth, then sallies to capture prey; stays close to cover. Difficult to see, but easily located by distinctive call. May eat some berries, especially in late summer.

Voice: High-pitched, rising, slurred *suweeet* call; three-part song of thin, squeaky notes heard less frequently.

Did you know? Pacific-slope Flycatcher is distinguishable only by call from the closely-related Cordilleran Flycatcher of the interior West.

Date & Location Seen: _____

Western Kingbird

Eastern Kingbird

WESTERN KINGBIRD / EASTERN KINGBIRD
Tyrannus verticalis / Tyrannus tyrannus

Description: 8½". Large-headed with **upright stance**, square-tipped, fairly long tail, pointed black bill. WESTERN: Grayish upper breast, **yellow belly**, greenish-gray back, **black tail with white edges**. EASTERN: **White below**, dark-gray above, **white tail tip**.

Similar Species: Olive-sided Flycatcher (page 233) smaller with short tail, vested appearance. Tropical Kingbird (not shown; rare fall visitor in Region) similar to Western but tail forked, lacks white edges.

Seasonal Abundance: Both uncommon to rare in Region, late May–August. WESTERN: Breeds western North America from southern Canada to northern Mexico, winters southern Mexico to Costa Rica. EASTERN: Breeds from Washington, British Columbia across North America, south to Texas, Florida; winters in western Amazon Basin.

Where to Find: Lowlands; have bred in Skagit Valley. Transients may appear anywhere in open areas. WESTERN: Most likely in May, has nested on South Sound Prairies. EASTERN: Has nested at Spencer Island.

Habitat: Fields, open rural areas with trees, structures for nesting, often near water.

Diet and Behavior: Forage from prominent perches, flying out to capture insects; also eat fruit.

Voice: Vocal at nest; transients seldom call. WESTERN: Call sharp *kit*. EASTERN: Rapid twittering notes.

Did you know? Both species are aggressive toward intruders near their nests, often attacking much larger birds.

Date & Location Seen: _____

Description: 9½″. Large-headed, long-tailed songbird, mostly pearl-gray; **wings, tail, mask black. White marks** in wing, outer tail visible in flight. **Bill large** with slight hook. Immature browner, dark markings less distinct; scaling below.

Similar Species: Loggerhead Shrike (not shown; extremely rare in Region) smaller with heavier mask that crosses over base of its smaller bill.

Seasonal Abundance: Uncommon resident in Region, October to early April. Breeds on tundra around northern hemisphere, winters to temperate zone.

Where to Find: Lowlands to lower foothills; migrants may appear in open areas within cities. Good locations include Skagit, Samish Flats, Nisqually National Wildlife Refuge.

Habitat: Fields, coastal marshes, other open places with scattered trees, bushes.

Diet and Behavior: Preys on small mammals, birds, insects by perching prominently, often at highest point of shrub, then swooping down, dispatching victim with bill. Often impales food on thorn or barbed wire in sheltered location to facilitate feeding or store for later use. Flight slightly undulating with rapid flapping, halting pauses.

Voice: Occasionally offers mellow, warbled phrases of song in winter quarters.

Did you know? Northern Shrikes, often called butcher birds, appear in variable numbers each winter dependent on reproductive success and food supply in the far north.

Date & Location Seen: _____

Description: 5¹/2″. Compact with short tail, heavy bill. Grayish-green above with **grayer head**, white below with yellowish flanks. Prominent **white wing-bars, bold well-defined white spectacles**.

Similar Species: Hutton's Vireo (page 249) head rounder, diffuse eye-ring broken at top. Other vireos in Region lack wing-bars. Red-eyed Vireo (page 253) song sweeter with complex phrases.

Seasonal Abundance: Uncommon resident in Region mid-April to September. Ranges in West from British Columbia to California, winters Mexico.

Where to Find: Local breeder in lowlands throughout Region. Good bets include San Juan Islands, forested locations in Skagit, Pierce, Kitsap counties. Migrants widespead anywhere with trees, including urban locations.

Habitat: Mixed, coniferous forests. Migrants use woodland edge, parks, neighborhoods.

Diet and Behavior: Forages sluggishly, deliberately in upper canopy for insects, some small fruits. Inconspicuous unless singing; may sing less frequently than other vireos. Joins mixed flocks in migration.

Voice: Song loud, consisting of simple, slurred, burry whistles with pauses between notes tending to be longer than notes themselves. Calls include series of harsh, falling *shep* notes.

Did you know? Cassin's Vireo is the westernmost of three closely-related species long classified as a single species, the Solitary Vireo. The other two are Plumbeous Vireo of the interior West and Blue-headed Vireo of the East.

Date & Location Seen: _____

Description: 4³/4″. Small, compact, **greenish-gray** above, lighter below with **white wing-bars**. Prominent, **diffuse white eye-ring** broken above eye, extending forward to thick, stubby bill. **Feet bluish-gray**.

Similar Species: Ruby-crowned Kinglet (page 295) almost identical, smaller with thin bill, yellowish feet, black below lower wing-bar. Tends to flick wings more often. Male kinglet's red crown may be hidden. Cassin's Vireo (page 247) larger with longer bill, well-defined spectacled appearance.

Seasonal Abundance: Fairly common but often overlooked resident in Region. Ranges from southwestern British Columbia down coast to California, also mountains from southeastern Arizona, southwestern Texas to Central America.

Where to Find: Lowlands to moderate elevations in foothills. Inconspicuous if not vocalizing. Typical sites include Discovery Park (Seattle), Watershed Park (Olympia), Foulweather Bluff Preserve (Kitsap County).

Habitat: Mixed woodlands, forest edge, thickets.

Diet and Behavior: Forages deliberately, mostly for insects, but takes some berries. Found often in pairs. Males sing constantly during brief period late winter–early spring. Joins mixed-species foraging flocks outside nesting season.

Voice: Song simple, slurred, whistled phrase repeated monotonously. Varied calls include rising *bree dee dee*, harsh mewing.

Did you know? Most vireos live in the tropics or migrate there for the winter. Hutton's is the only vireo to remain year round so far north.

Date & Location Seen: _____

Description: 5¼″. More compact than warblers. **Plain grayish-green above**, whitish below. **Prominent light eyebrow** only distinguishing mark. Sometimes erects crest in excitement. JUVENILE: Yellower below.

Similar Species: Red-eyed Vireo (page 253) larger with longer bill, gray cap, eyebrow bordered with black above, below. Other vireos have wing-bars. Warblers yellower, thinner-billed.

Seasonal Abundance: Common resident in Region, May–September. Breeds from extreme southeastern Alaska to Maine, south in mountains to central Mexico; winters Mexico to northern Central America.

Where to Find: Widespread breeder from sea level to mountain passes except uncommon in urban areas. Common migrant throughout Region.

Habitat: Breeds in mixed open woodland, forest edge, aspen groves. Also found in mostly coniferous woods, but utilizes available broadleaf trees for nesting.

Diet and Behavior: Forages mostly in deciduous growth, primarily for insects; also some berries. Joins mixed flocks in migration. Sings often, even in migration, but difficult to spot due to slow foraging style.

Voice: Song extended, languid, rambling warble, different from other vireos – reminiscent of Purple Finch. Calls include nasal mewing.

Did you know? Vireos weave cup-shaped nests suspended from horizontal forked branches, sometimes placed at fairly low height.

Date & Location Seen: _____

Description: 5¾″. Compact, short-tailed. Large, flat-looking head with heavy black bill. **Plain-greenish above** except for **gray cap**; whitish below. **White eyebrow bordered with black line above, another below** passing through red eye. Sometimes erects crest in excitement. JUVENILE: Brown eye.

Similar Species: Warbling Vireo (page 251) smaller with shorter bill, lacks gray cap, black lines bordering eyebrow. Other vireos have wing-bars; warblers smaller.

Seasonal Abundance: Fairly common resident in Region, late May–August. North American population breeds across Canada, Northwest, East, winters in Amazon Basin. Other races resident in South America.

Where to Find: Nests locally in lowlands, mostly in major river valleys; rare migrant away from breeding sites. Best bets Skagit Valley near Rockport, Snoqualmie Valley above Carnation.

Habitat: Prefers mature broadleaf woods, especially cottonwood groves along rivers. Also forests, parks with mature maple groves.

Diet and Behavior: Forages mostly in canopy, primarily on insects, but also eats berries (especially in fall). Sings persistently, but difficult to spot due to slow foraging style.

Voice: Song continuous, short but complex; low, whistled phrases given every couple of seconds. Calls include mewed *nyeeah*.

Did you know? Red-eyed Vireos have been observed singing while sitting on their nests.

Date & Location Seen: _____

Steller's Jay

Western Scrub-Jay

Description: 12". Both mostly **blue, long-tailed**. STELLER'S: Blue except upper body blackish, **long, prominent crest**, black banding on tail, wings. SCRUB: **No crest**, blue above with brown back patch, white eyebrow, dark cheek; **white below with partial blue breast band**.

Similar Species: None in Region.

Seasonal Abundance: STELLER'S: Fairly common resident in Region but scarce breeder in cities, possibly impacted by crows. Ranges in West from Alaska to Nicaragua. SCRUB: Uncommon but increasing resident in southern part of Region, rare in northern part. Ranges from Washington to Colorado, south to Mexico.

Where to Find: STELLER'S: Throughout Region to tree line. SCRUB: Lowland open areas with thick brush, mostly neighborhoods.

Habitat: STELLER'S: Coniferous but also mixed woods. SCRUB: Open woods, gardens, farms, often near oaks.

Diet and Behavior: Both species omnivorous, eat more seeds in fall, winter, visit bird feeders. Secretive when nesting. STELLER'S: Gregarious, often in small groups; forages higher in trees but also to ground. SCRUB: Forages more on ground or in brush; usually found in pairs, family groups.

Voice: Both species noisy with frequent contact calls. Most common calls: STELLER'S: Harsh *shaark shaark shraak*. SCRUB: Harsh, higher-pitched, rising *sheeeenk*.

Did you know? Jays are among the most intelligent birds.

Date & Location Seen: _____

Description: 16". Chunky, but shape can vary in flight. **Completely black** with stout bill, **short, square, fan-shaped tail**. JUVENILE: Brownish-black with red mouth lining.

Similar Species: Common Raven (page 259) larger with wedge-shaped tail, longer bill, different voice; soars more, with wings held flat.

Seasonal Abundance: Common resident in Region. Ranges across North America from central Canada to southern U.S.

Where to Find: Abundant in cities, towns, agricultural areas, river valleys; less common in more remote areas of dense coniferous forest, high mountains.

Habitat: Open woodlands, fields, clearings, cities, wherever trees available for nesting.

Diet and Behavior: Omnivorous, eating anything available. Feeds on refuse, handouts, road kills, crops, fruit, seeds, insects. Intelligent, highly gregarious; forms huge night roosts after nesting season, sometimes numbering in thousands. Harasses predators noisily until they vacate crow territory or remain motionless in cover.

Voice: Noisy, garrulous. Common call *caww*.

Did you know? Crows in our area are currently classified as two species, American Crow and Northwestern Crow. The latter is supposed to be smaller and more coastal. Many ornithologists, however, maintain that there is really only one species since the two forms interbreed freely and are nearly indistinguishable.

Date & Location Seen: _____

Description: 24". **Largest songbird**, with wingspan over four feet. **Entirely glossy-black** with long wings, **long, wedge-shaped tail, long, heavy, formidable bill**. Puffy throat, head feathers erected in display impart even larger look.

Similar Species: American Crow (page 257) smaller with shorter bill, different voice; lacks wedge-shaped tail. Ravens soar more often.

Seasonal Abundance: Fairly common resident in Region away from urban areas. Ranges across northern hemisphere from Arctic to temperate zone, south in mountains to Central America.

Where to Find: Throughout Region, except absent from Everett–Tacoma urban corridor. Apparently excluded by crows from cities.

Habitat: Coniferous, mixed forests; coastal, agricultural areas.

Diet and Behavior: Omnivorous, feeding on whatever available. Specializes in scavenging on large carcasses, descending on road kills, but also kills rodents, robs nests, feeds on insects. Highly intelligent, cautious; follows predators, hunters to take advantage of easy meal. Carries, hides food for future needs. Pairs, groups cavort in aerial displays.

Voice: Varied calls include harsh croak, liquid bell-like sounds, screamed *kraaah*, metallic rattles.

Did you know? Crows and ravens are always at odds. Ravens raid crow nests. Crows often swoop down on ravens while attempting to chase them away.

Date & Location Seen: _____

Male

Female

Description: 8". **Large**, long-winged swallow with **shallowly-forked tail**, relatively large bill. MALE: Adult **entirely dark-purplish-blue**. First-year male resembles female with some blue below. FEMALE: **Gray of throat, chest extends around neck** in collar; belly dingy-whitish; back, tail, face all-dark.

Similar Species: Larger than other swallows, soars more. European Starling (page 307) stubby with shorter tail. Black Swift (page 215) with longer, thinner, curving wings, more flickering wing-beat.

Seasonal Abundance: Fairly common resident in Region mid-April to September. Ranges throughout eastern North America west to prairie provinces, West Coast south from British Columbia; also locally in interior West. Winters in South America.

Where to Find: Quite local at scattered coastal locations (e.g., Shilshole Bay, Port Ludlow); also Joint Base Lewis-McChord.

Habitat: Open areas, mostly near water.

Diet and Behavior: Forages in flight for insects. Flocks in migration, sometimes with other swallows. Nests in small colonies, mostly in boxes, gourds provided by humans. Competes with other cavity nesters; sharply declined with European Starling introduction, but martins succeed in nest sites over water, often on pilings.

Voice: Song low-pitched, liquid warbles. Calls include rich, descending *cher cher*, rattle in alarm.

Did you know? Eastern Purple Martin populations are highly colonial, using multi-unit nest structures. Western populations are only loosely colonial, shunning multi-unit boxes.

Date & Location Seen: _____

Male

Female First-year

Description: 5¾". Relatively stocky. Broad, triangular wings; short, slightly-notched tail. **Glossy, iridescent-blue above, bright-white underparts**. FEMALE: Duller, with brown upperparts in first year changing to blue with age. JUVENILE: Plain-brown above.

Similar Species: Violet-green Swallow (page 265) greener with white "saddlebag" flank patches, white cheek extending above eye. Juveniles difficult to separate. Northern Rough-winged Swallow (page 267) has dusky throat, upper breast.

Seasonal Abundance: Common summer resident in Region, arrives by February, begins to depart by July, most gone before September. Rare in winter. Breeds from Alaska to Labrador south through most of U.S., winters southern U.S., West Indies, Mexico, Central America.

Where to Find: Widespread but local at mostly low or moderate elevation, usually near water.

Habitat: Open areas near water with trees, boxes for nest sites.

Diet and Behavior: Forages in flight for insects. Eats some berries during migration, winter. Forms large flocks in migration, sometimes with other swallows. Nests in pairs but also in loose colonies, using natural cavities, nest boxes. Competes with other species for nest sites.

Voice: Song composed of series of chirps, warbles. Calls include liquid *chweet*, chattering in alarm.

Did you know? The Tree Swallow is the only songbird species in which one-year-old females have a different, distinct immature plumage.

Date & Location Seen: _____

Male

Male

VIOLET-GREEN SWALLOW
Tachycineta thalassina

Description: 5¼". Fairly **petite**, long-winged, with slightly-notched tail. **White below**, including **saddlebag-like flank patches**. MALE: Glossy, iridescent purple-green above with **white extending above eye**. FEMALE: Duller; bronze-green with gray wash below, duskier cheek. JUVENILE: Lacks green.

Similar Species: Tree Swallow (page 263) bluer, with dark cheek, flanks.

Seasonal Abundance: Common summer resident in Region, begins to return by late February, departs by October. Breeds in West from Alaska to Mexico; winters Mexico, northern Central America.

Where to Find: Widespread, from coast up to fairly high elevations.

Habitat: Open areas including woodlands, cities, agricultural lands; often near water in migration.

Diet and Behavior: Forages in flight for insects, often at great height. Forms large flocks in migration, sometimes with other swallows. Nests in pairs but may be found in small colonies, nesting in cliff crevices, under building eaves, or in natural cavities, nest boxes. Scouts openings in buildings for potential nest sites.

Voice: Song repeated *tsip tseet tsip*, reminiscent of Pine Siskin. Calls include *chilip* – higher, sharper than Tree Swallow.

Did you know? Male Violet-green Swallows sing their courtship song monotonously in the pre-dawn darkness.

Date & Location Seen: _____

NORTHERN ROUGH-WINGED SWALLOW
Stelgidopteryx serripennis

Description: 5¾". Bulkier than most swallows, with smooth, deep wing-beats, square tail. **Plain-brownish above**, whitish below, with **dingy gray throat, upper breast**. JUVENILE: Cinnamon on wings.

Similar Species: Cliff Swallow (page 269) has rusty-orange rump, white forehead spot. Female Purple Martin (page 261) larger, tail forked. Bank Swallow (not shown; rare in Region) smaller with white throat, distinct brown breast band. Other white-bellied swallows have white throats.

Seasonal Abundance: Fairly common resident in Region, April–August; a few linger to September. Breeds across North America from southern Alaska to Maritimes, south through Central America; northern populations move south in winter.

Where to Find: Throughout Region, mostly at lower elevations.

Habitat: Open areas, usually near water, especially cut stream banks.

Diet and Behavior: Forages in flight low over water, fields for insects. Less likely to flock than other swallows, but joins mixed groups of swallows. Not colonial nester, but favorable site may attract more than one pair. Uses old burrow nests of other species, culvert pipe, other tubular man-made structures. Sometimes digs nest burrow.

Voice: Song rough, repeated *frrep*. Call harsh, low *breet*.

Did you know? The "rough-winged" moniker comes from the small serrations this species shows on its wing feathers.

Date & Location Seen: _____

Description: 5½". Compact swallow with **square, dark tail, rusty-buff rump. Dark-chestnut throat, cheek** contrast with whitish underparts. **Light forehead spot**, buff collar stand out from dark cap, dark back streaked with white. Long, dark, pointed wings, tiny feet, bill.

Similar Species: Other swallows lack orange-buff rump.

Seasonal Abundance: Common resident in Region, April–August; a few linger to September. Breeds across North America from Arctic to Mexico, winters in South America.

Where to Find: Widespread in open lowlands, ranging up some river drainages into mountains.

Habitat: Open areas, often near water; nests on cliffs or man-made structures, preferably of concrete, such as bridges, dams, buildings.

Diet and Behavior: Forages in flight for insects. Flocks at all seasons, nests in colonies. Each pair builds gourd-shaped nest on vertical surface with some overhead protection, using mud pellets. Enters nest through short, narrow tunnel. Stages in large numbers away from nest sites when young fledge, then departs for South America.

Voice: Song thin, harsh twitters, given in series. Calls include husky *churr*, soft, low *veew* given in alarm.

Did you know? Other birds use Cliff Swallow nests for roosting in winter.

Date & Location Seen: _____

Description: 7″. **Streamlined**, graceful in flight. Blue-black above, **long, forked tail** with white spot near tip of each tail feather. Long, dark, pointed wings. **Cinnamon-buff below** with dark breast band, rusty throat, forehead, small black bill. Perches upright with tiny feet. JUVENILE: Pale beneath without tail streamers.

Similar Species: Other swallows lack forked tail. Purple Martin (page 261) larger, tail less forked.

Seasonal Abundance: Common resident in Region, mid-April to mid-September; migrants continue through October. Rare in winter. Breeds around northern hemisphere from Arctic to subtropical zone; winters to southern hemisphere, mostly in tropics.

Where to Find: Throughout Region; most common near man-made structures.

Habitat: Open habitats with buildings, bridges, culverts for nesting. Tends to be near water in migration.

Diet and Behavior: Forages in flight for insects. Flocks in migration, often with other swallows. Builds nest from mud, grasses, lined with feathers, often inside or beneath structures, choosing mostly horizontal but also vertical surfaces.

Voice: Song string of squeaky, twittering notes, grating sounds. Calls include *vit*, emphatic *pit veet* given in alarm.

Did you know? The Barn Swallow has adapted nearly completely to nesting on man-made structures. Nests built on natural sites such as shallow caves and crevices are rarely found.

Date & Location Seen: _____

Description: 5¼". Typical chickadee, with **white cheek dividing dark cap from black bib**. Small, thin bill. **Cap black**, belly white, sides buffy, wings, tail, **back gray**. Puget Sound populations duskier than birds east of Cascades.

Similar Species: Chestnut-backed Chickadee (page 275) smaller with sooty-brown cap, chestnut sides, back. Mountain Chickadee (page 379) has white eyebrow.

Seasonal Abundance: Common resident in Region. Ranges from Alaska to Newfoundland, south to New Mexico, Tennessee.

Where to Find: Throughout Region although absent from higher elevations. Scarce on San Juan Islands.

Habitat: Broadleaf, mixed woods, thickets, neighborhoods. Prefers deciduous growth, especially alders.

Diet and Behavior: Searches for insects, seeds among branches, hanging upside down to glean leaf undersides. Highly sociable when not nesting – forms small flocks, joins mixed flocks. Uses cavities, nest boxes, sometimes in backyards. Visits bird feeders, storing seeds in tree bark nearby.

Voice: Song clear whistle. Core Puget Sound populations give 3–6 note *fee fee fee fee fee*. Populations away from Sound more typical of species, high *fee beee*, with lower second note. Calls include *chick a dee dee dee*.

Did you know? Chickadees are capable of going into a night torpor, which saves energy.

Date & Location Seen: _____

Description: 4¾″. Typical chickadee with **white cheek dividing dark cap from black bib. Cap sooty-brown; sides, back rich-chestnut**; small, thin bill, grayish wings, tail.

Similar Species: Black-capped Chickadee (page 273) slightly larger with black cap, lacks chestnut color. Mountain Chickadee (page 379) with white eyebrow, also lacks chestnut.

Seasonal Abundance: Common resident in Region. Ranges from south-central Alaska to central California, mostly along coast, but inland across Washington, southern British Columbia to northwestern Montana.

Where to Find: Throughout Region from just below tree line to coast, including cities.

Habitat: Coniferous forest; also mixed woods, but seldom far from conifers. Dispersing birds in fall may use deciduous woodlands.

Diet and Behavior: Forages among branches for insects, seeds, some berries, hanging upside down while gleaning on twigs. May form larger flocks than Black-capped; flocks with it, other species. Uses cavities, nest boxes, sometimes in backyards. Visits bird feeders, often storing seeds in tree bark nearby.

Voice: *Chick zee zee* call higher, hoarser than other chickadees in Region. Lacks whistled song of Black-capped.

Did you know? Historically the most abundant Puget Sound chickadee, the Chestnut-backed is now outnumbered by the Black-capped in many areas where conifers have been replaced by broadleaf vegetation.

Date & Location Seen: _____

Male

Female

Description: 4″. **Tiny, plain-grayish, nondescript** but lighter underneath, browner on head with **long tail**. Bill tiny, blackish, slightly downcurved. Eye white in female, dark in male, juvenile.

Similar Species: Chickadees have white cheek patches. Kinglets have wing-bars, shorter tails.

Seasonal Abundance: Common resident in Region at lower elevations. Ranges in West from southwestern British Columbia to Guatemala.

Where to Find: Throughout lowlands, following some river drainages into mountains; numerous in urban areas.

Habitat: Broadleaf, mixed woodlands, open forest, parks, neighborhoods.

Diet and Behavior: Forages in flocks except during short period while nesting. Groups of up to fifty individuals move from tree to tree in tight line, almost in single file. Feeds mostly on insects but may eat seeds, berries. Visits suet feeders. Builds extraordinary hanging nest woven of moss, lichen, spider web, other materials, up to a foot long with small entrance near top, usually less than ten feet from ground.

Voice: Calls given by flocking birds include short *tsip*, trilled alarm call.

Did you know? Bushtits are the smallest North American birds by weight except for the hummingbirds.

Date & Location Seen: _____

Description: 4¼". **Stubby-tailed**, with straight, chisel-like bill. Gray above, **rusty underneath, white eyebrow** separates black cap from **black eye-line**. MALE: Brighter than female, juvenile.

Similar Species: Among other bark-clinging birds, Brown Creeper (page 281) streaked above, woodpeckers much larger. Chickadees have longer tails, white cheek patch.

Seasonal Abundance: Common resident in Region. Numbers variably increase in lowland urban areas due to migration, downslope movement in winter. Breeds in conifer-forest zones across Canada, northern, western U.S. Winters south to Florida, Texas some years.

Where to Find: Throughout Region from tree line to coast, including urban areas.

Habitat: Coniferous, mixed forests, parks, woodlots.

Diet and Behavior: Acrobatically climbs up, down tree trunks in search of insect prey, mostly in summer. More dependant on seeds in winter, particularly from conifers; may migrate from areas without adequate cone crop. Excavates nest cavity in rotten wood. Joins mixed-species flocks outside nesting season. Regular at sunflower, suet bird feeders.

Voice: Calls include short nasal *enk* given in series.

Did you know? Red-breasted Nuthatches smear conifer sap around their nest holes to deter predators.

Date & Location Seen: _____

Description: 5¼". Slim, **streaked brownish-gray above** except for plain-rusty rump, **white eyebrow**; white below, brightest on chin, breast. **Hitches up tree trunks** with long, stiff tail. Bill long, thin, downcurved.

Similar Species: Red-breasted Nuthatch (page 279) unstreaked, reddish below. Woodpeckers much larger. Bewick's Wren (page 289) sometimes goes up trees; has more-uniform, brown upperparts, longer, free-wheeling tail.

Seasonal Abundance: Fairly common resident throughout Region. Some downslope movement occurs in winter. Breeds in forest zones from Alaska to Labrador, Middle Atlantic states, south through western U.S. to Central America. Some winter across rest of continent to northeastern Mexico.

Where to Find: Throughout Region to mountain passes, including urban areas.

Habitat: Forests, open groves, parks containing good-sized trees.

Diet and Behavior: Forages for insects while hitching up bark of tree using tail as brace. Probes crevices as it climbs, then flies down low onto next tree, begins again. Builds nest under sheets of loose bark on trunks, large branches. Joins mixed-species flocks outside nesting season.

Voice: Song high-pitched rising, falling notes in series, often ending on high note. Call high, thin *tseee*.

Did you know? The sight of the Brown Creeper's white breast as it moves up the tree may cause prey to move, facilitating detection.

Date & Location Seen: _____

Description: 4¾″. **Nondescript plain-brown, paler below**, with **thin bill**. Fine, dark banding on wings, tail, vague line through eye. **Light eye-ring**. Often holds tail at upward angle.

Similar Species: Bewick's Wren (page 289) larger, with bold white eyebrow. Pacific Wren (page 285) darker, with short tail. Marsh Wren (page 287) in wet habitat, with whitish eyebrow, streaks on back; plain juveniles difficult to separate.

Seasonal Abundance: Fairly common but highly local summer resident in Region. Northern populations breed across southern Canada, most of U.S., winter southern U.S., Mexico. Other forms resident Mexico to South America, often considered separate species.

Where to Find: Most common in San Juan Islands, South Sound Prairies, Whidbey Island, but rare in most of Region. Joint Base Lewis-McChord, Fort Casey State Park good bets.

Habitat: Drier forest edge, semi-open habitats at lower elevations including clearcuts, areas near human habitation.

Diet and Behavior: Forages on ground, bushes for insects. Nests in cavities, including nest boxes. Competes for nest sites with other species. Males vigorously protect territory with constant singing.

Voice: Song exuberant, bubbling trills, whistled notes, given in rapid series. Calls include scolding, rattling, nasal mewing.

Did you know? The male House Wren fills many prospective nest holes with materials and the female lays eggs in one.

Date & Location Seen: _____

Description: 4". **Tiny, round, with stubby tail**, thin bill, light-brown eyebrow. Chocolate-brown above, **fine, dark banding on tail, wings, belly. Breast rich rufous-brown**. Secretive but constantly active.

Similar Species: Bewick's Wren (page 289) larger, with bold white eyebrow. House Wren (page 283) with light breast. Marsh Wren (page 287) with whitish eyebrow, streaked back.

Seasonal Abundance: Common resident in Region; lowland numbers increase in winter. Breeds in conifer-forest zones from Alaska to central California, east to Rockies; winters in breeding range, southwestern U.S.

Where to Find: Throughout Region. Breeds to mountain passes, withdraws to below level of heavy snow in winter. Frequent then in neighborhoods, parks, but tends to breed away from urbanization.

Habitat: Nests in wet underbrush of coniferous forest. Dense forest, thickets, tangles in winter, migration.

Diet and Behavior: Moves mouse-like through low undergrowth, eating insects; may also eat berries. Investigates intruders from open perch while bobbing up-and-down. Males sing from low, hidden or mid-level, exposed perches.

Voice: Song remarkable lengthy series of varied tinkling trills, warbles. Calls include oft-given *chit chit*, rapid, staccato series of chips.

Did you know? Pacific Wren has recently been elevated to full species status, distinct from Winter Wren of eastern North America and Eurasian Wren.

Date & Location Seen: _____

Description: 4¾″. **Secretive** but curious. Brown above with **fine dark banding on wings, tail**, plain-grayish below; **tail held cocked up**. Dark cap, white eyebrow, faint white streaks on upper back. Long, thin bill curves down. JUVENILE: Appears almost plain-brown with vague light eyebrow.

Similar Species: House Wren (page 283) plainer with only very faint eyebrow. Bewick's Wren (page 289) larger, with bolder white eyebrow. Pacific Wren (page 285) darker, with short tail.

Seasonal Abundance: Common resident in Region, less so in winter. Breeds across continent from British Columbia to New England, south to California, Gulf Coast (but absent in interior Southeast); winters south to Mexico.

Where to Find: Widespread throughout Region at lower elevations, in appropriate habitat.

Habitat: Open freshwater or brackish marshes with thick emergent vegetation, usually cattails. Also salt marshes, river edge, wet fields, scrub adjacent to wetlands.

Diet and Behavior: Forages low, crawling within thick cover, mostly for insects. Male sings day or night from exposed or hidden perches with tail cocked, often flat against back.

Voice: Song mechanical but musical rattled trill begun with a few call notes. Call distinctive *tik*.

Did you know? The male Marsh Wren builds multiple spherical nests amidst emergent stalks; the female chooses one to line and lay eggs in.

Date & Location Seen: _____

Description: 5¼". Slim, **plain-brown**, with **bold white eyebrow**, long, thin down-curved bill, **long, brown tail** with fine dark bands above, **black-and-white edging, undersurface**. Often flicks tail from side to side.

Similar Species: House Wren (page 283), Marsh Wren (page 287) with much fainter eyebrows. Pacific Wren (page 285) tiny, darker, with stubby tail.

Seasonal Abundance: Common resident in Region. Ranges from southwestern British Columbia to California, across southwestern states to Texas, Mexico; spottily distributed east of Mississippi River.

Where to Find: Widespread in lowlands, including cities. Frequent in backyards.

Habitat: Forest edge, open habitats at lower elevations including hedgerows, thickets, areas near human habitation.

Diet and Behavior: Forages mostly for insects, some berries in dense undergrowth, but also probes bark on larger limbs, feeds on ground. Nests in thickets or cavities, often in man-made objects.

Voice: Song extremely variable, loud series of warbles, ringing trills, beginning with soft buzz that sounds like inhalation; easily confused with Song Sparrow. Calls numerous, including scolding, harsh notes, sharp *jik*.

Did you know? Bewick's Wren was once more common and widespread in eastern North America than in the West. For unknown reasons the situation has reversed in recent decades, as eastern populations have continued to decline sharply while western populations expand.

Date & Location Seen: _____

Description: 7½". Stout, **chunky, uniform slate-gray, with short tail**, thin, straight bill, pale legs. Shape, **bobbing motions** suggest large wren. Often flashes white eyelids. JUVENILE: Spotted breast.

Similar Species: Distinctive; much larger than any wren in Region.

Seasonal Abundance: Uncommon resident in Region, mostly mountains, foothills in summer; may be seen in more urbanized areas in winter. Ranges in western mountains from Aleutians to Central America.

Where to Find: During nesting season, rushing streams (less frequently ponds) from middle elevations up to tree line. Moves downstream in winter to larger rivers, suburban creeks. Good bets then Dungeness River Fish Hatchery, Skagit River east of Rockport.

Habitat: Rushing streams, rivers, pond margins. Occasional at stream mouths in winter.

Diet and Behavior: Swims or walks on stream bottoms in pursuit of aquatic insect larvae, mollusks, small fish, fish eggs. Stands, bobs on streamside rocks, flying up, down stream to feed, protect territory. Builds bulky, domed nests next to streams, often under bridges. Uses wings to "fly" underwater.

Voice: Song loud, piercing musical whistles repeated in series. Calls include buzzy *bzzeet*.

Did you know? Dippers are the only true aquatic songbirds.

Date & Location Seen: _____

Description: 3¾". Tiny, with **short, notched tail**, thin bill, constant, **nervous wing-flitting**. Olive-gray above, grayish-white below, **white wing-bars, dark flight feathers with golden edging**. Broad **white eyebrow below black-striped crown**. Crown center orange-and-yellow in male, yellow in female; colors may be obscured.

Similar Species: Ruby-crowned Kinglet (page 295) slightly larger, greener; has eye-ring, no head stripes. Warblers larger.

Seasonal Abundance: Common resident in Region. Breeds in conifer-forest zones from southeastern Alaska across continent to Newfoundland, south in mountains to Guatemala; winters through all but northernmost parts of breeding range south across U.S. to northeastern Mexico.

Where to Find: Throughout Region including lowlands, mountains, cities.

Habitat: Breeds in conifer stands, winters in mixed woods; migrants appear anywhere.

Diet and Behavior: Forages high, low, although when nesting tends to remain high. Gregarious when not nesting. Prefers conifers but seeks out insects in low deciduous growth, climbing, gleaning, hanging upside down, moving rapidly in flocks. Joins mixed flocks.

Voice: Song begins with three high, thin notes, ends with tumbling chatter. Call thin *tsee tsee tsee* or *tsee*.

Did you know? The English and Latin names of kinglets reflect the jeweled crowns and assertive behavior of these "little kings".

Date & Location Seen: _____

Description: 4″. **Tiny, plump-appearing, with short tail**, thin bill, constant, **nervous wing-flitting**. Greenish-gray above, lighter below. **Dark wings with white wing-bars**, blackish below lower bar. Prominent but diffuse **white eye-ring**. Red crown of male usually obscured.

Similar Species: Golden-crowned Kinglet (page 293) has light eyebrow below black stripe, no eye-ring. Hutton's Vireo (page 249) very similar but larger with thicker bill, blue-gray not yellowish feet; lacks black below wing-bar.

Seasonal Abundance: Common migrant, winter resident in lowlands of Region, September to mid-May. Nests high in Cascades, Olympics on fringes of Region. Breeding range from Alaska, British Columbia to Labrador, south in mountains of West; winters Pacific Coast, southern states to Guatemala.

Where to Find: Winters throughout lowlands in urban, agricultural settings, remote areas. Up to mountain passes in migration.

Habitat: Breeds in coniferous forest; prefers thickets, brush, forest edge in winter.

Diet and Behavior: Forages low or high, mostly for insects. Eats some berries. Congregates in attractive habitats. Joins mixed-species flocks.

Voice: Song long, rolling series of trills, twitters, repeated phrases, often heard in spring migration. Call low, husky *jidit*.

Did you know? Curious and easily attracted, male Ruby-crowned Kinglets display their red crowns aggressively when agitated.

Date & Location Seen: _____

Lazuli Bunting
Male

Male

Female

Description: 6¾". Small, **upright thrush** with short, thin bill, **solid-blue wings, tail**. MALE: Bright-blue above with **rusty-brown breast**, gray belly. FEMALE: Less blue; back, head grayish, breast pale-rust. JUVENILE: Grayer with vague speckling, **whitish eye-ring**.

Similar Species: Mountain Bluebird (page 379) usually lacks rusty tones on breast. Male **Lazuli Bunting** (see inset; rare in Region in similar habitats) smaller with **white wing-bars, finch-like bill**.

Seasonal Abundance: Uncommon summer resident in Region. Becomes rare by winter, returns early March. Ranges from British Columbia to highlands of Mexico; northern populations move south in winter.

Where to Find: Lowlands, foothills. Highest density in South Sound Prairies; thinly distributed in clearcuts, farmlands throughout Region. Best bet Joint Base Lewis-McChord; rare but regular in Clallam, Mason, Thurston counties.

Habitat: Meadows, clearcuts with standing snags, farms, open woods.

Diet and Behavior: Forages mostly on insects, also berries, especially after summer. Hunts from low perch over short grass, may hover before capture. Flocks outside nesting season. Cavity nester; readily accepts nest boxes mounted at open sites near ground.

Voice: Seldom sings. Calls include low, chattering, whistled *chwer*.

Did you know? Bluebirds returned to the Joint Base Lewis-McChord prairies thanks to an extensive nest-box campaign. Active management is necessary, however, to maintain open habitat.

Date & Location Seen: _____

Description: 6³/₄″. **Plain warm-brown above** from head to tail. Buff breast with small dark spots. Thin bill, brown face with diffuse, **buffy eye-ring** extending to bill, giving **spectacled appearance**.

Similar Species: Hermit Thrush (page 301) with contrasting rusty tail, thin white eye-ring, habit of cocking tail. Juvenile American Robin (page 303) much larger, some orange on breast.

Seasonal Abundance: Common summer resident throughout Region to mountain passes. Breeds from Alaska across Canada, northern states to Newfoundland, south to California in West. Winters from Mexico to South America.

Where to Find: Throughout Region, mid-May to early September; a few linger later. Mostly breeds away from urbanized areas. Migrants secretive but widespread.

Habitat: Leafy deciduous or mixed woods, often near streams. Prefers dense understory cover with salmonberry, other native shrubs.

Diet and Behavior: Forages on ground but also often in trees, unlike Hermit Thrush. Feeds on insects, berries. Migrates at night.

Voice: Song – series of nasal whistles spiraling upward – may be mistaken for that of Purple Finch. Calls include low, whistled *whit*.

Did you know? Swainson's Thrushes in the Puget Sound Region belong to a distinctive race sometimes called Russet-backed Thrush. A different race, the Olive-backed Thrush, is found in eastern Washington.

Date & Location Seen: _____

Description: 6¾". **Plain grayish-brown upperparts contrast with reddish-brown rump, tail**. Buffy-white breast with dark spots, gray flanks. Thin bill, **thin white eye-ring** on brownish face. Head grayish or brownish dependent on race.

Similar Species: Swainson's Thrush (page 299) lacks reddish tail; rarely cocks tail. Puget Sound population browner. Fox Sparrow (page 335) with conical bill.

Seasonal Abundance: Fairly common breeder at higher elevations in Region. Common but secretive migrant, uncommon winter resident in lowlands. Breeds across continent from Alaska to Newfoundland; winters coasts, southern U.S., south to Central America.

Where to Find: Breeds in Cascades, Olympics, Black Hills. Winters in lowlands; migrants widespread.

Habitat: Coniferous, mixed forests, including older, regenerating clearcuts. In winter, thickets, forest edge, parks, neighborhoods.

Diet and Behavior: Forages on or near ground for insects, fruit. Cocks, then slowly lowers tail while pumping wings, giving call note (unlike Swainson's Thrush). Seldom flocks, but may feed in fruiting shrubs with other species. Migrates at night.

Voice: Song consists of ethereal, spiraling whistles given at different pitches. Calls include rising *zhweeee*, muffled *chup*.

Did you know? Hermit Thrushes sometimes stir leaf litter with one foot to flush prey.

Date & Location Seen: _____

Male

Juvenile

Description: 10″. Bulky, with solid-gray back. **Upright stance.** Thin but fairly stout yellow bill, dark stripes on white throat, **dull-orange breast**, white undertail, **white marks above, below eye.** MALE: Darker, head blackish. FEMALE: Breast lighter orange. JUVENILE: Spotted breast.

Similar Species: Spotted Towhee (page 329) smaller with white belly. Other thrushes smaller, without orange breast.

Seasonal Abundance: Common resident in Region. Breeds across North America, south in mountains of Mexico; winters from southern part of breeding range south to Guatemala.

Where to Find: Ubiquitous. Backyards to mountains.

Habitat: Forests, cities, lawns, open areas. Nests wherever trees, structures present for nest placement, mud available for construction.

Diet and Behavior: Runs on ground or stands still while searching for insects, worms. Takes fruits from bushes, trees, ground. Winter flocks can number in thousands. Roosts communally at night in dense vegetation, often near fruit. May migrate if driven south by cold, but usually returns north as soon as temperature allows.

Voice: Song familiar lengthy, rich caroling, consisting of rising, falling phrases. Calls include *tuk tuk tuk*, sharp *piik* given in alarm, high, thin *sreep* in flight.

Did you know? The American Robin takes its name from an Old World flycatcher which is also orange-breasted, though not closely related.

Date & Location Seen: _____

Male

Female

Description: 9¹/₂″. **Chunky, with short tail, dark breast band, dark mask**, bill. **Orange eyebrow**, breast, throat, wing patches, broad wing-bars. MALE: **Bluish-gray**, cap to tail; breast band, mask black. FEMALE: Brownish-gray mask, upperparts, with faint breast band.

Similar Species: American Robin (page 303) with longer tail, no breast band.

Seasonal Abundance: Common resident in Region, now breeds almost exclusively in mountains due to fragmentation of lowland forests. Fairly common in lowlands by October, leaves in April. Breeding range extends from Alaska, Yukon to northern California; vacates high mountains, northern parts of range in winter as birds move downslope or farther south (as far as southern California).

Where to Find: Throughout Region, mountains in summer, below level of heavy snow in winter, including neighborhoods, parks.

Habitat: Moist coniferous forest with thick understory.

Diet and Behavior: Forages for insects, fruits in trees, on ground. Eats mostly fruit in winter, sometimes visits sunflower feeders; may congregate near madrone, ornamentals. Flocks less than robins, but gregarious at times in migration, winter. Male sings year round from high perches.

Voice: Song fairly long, ethereal, trilled whistle, repeated at different pitches after long pauses. Calls include *chup* similar to Hermit Thrush.

Did you know? Varied Thrushes wander regularly as far as the East Coast.

Date & Location Seen: _____

Breeding

Juvenile

Non-breeding

Description: 8". Chunky, with **short tail, long, thin, pointed bill**. Short tail, gliding habit impart **triangular appearance in flight**. BREEDING: Plain **iridescent-blackish** with minimal brown feather edging, **yellow bill**. NON-BREEDING: Heavy white spotting, prominent brown feather edging throughout; dark bill. JUVENILE: **Plain grayish-brown**, dark bill.

Similar Species: Western Meadowlark (page 353) with white outer tail feathers, yellow breast. Blackbirds with longer tails, more conical bills.

Seasonal Abundance: Common year-round resident in Region. Original range Eurasia; introduced in many other parts of world including North America, where now found from Alaska, Labrador to West Indies, Mexico.

Where to Find: Throughout Region. Abundant in urban, agricultural areas, scarce in mountains, dense forest.

Habitat: Disturbed habitats including cities, parks, open woods, farms.

Diet and Behavior: Probes ground for insects. Forages in trees, on ground for whatever food available, often flycatches like swallows. Highly gregarious, gathering in noisy flocks of thousands, especially at evening roosts. May nest several times per year, competing for nest cavities with native species. Sings year round from prominent perches, sometimes while flapping wings like wind-up toy.

Voice: Continuous series of squeaks, squawks, including mimicry of other species.

Did you know? Introduced in New York in 1890, European Starlings expanded across the continent, reaching Puget Sound in the 1950s.

Date & Location Seen: _____

307

Description: 6½″. **Slender**, sparrow-like, with **long, dark, white-edged tail**, long, thin bill. Plain gray-brown above with faint wing-bars, variably **streaked below**, mostly on buff-white upper breast. Light eyebrow, eye-ring, mustache mark. **Bobs tail while feeding**.

Similar Species: Thin bill, tail-bobbing habit separate pipits from sparrows.

Seasonal Abundance: Fairly common spring/fall migrant in Region. Breeds in mountains on alpine tundra. Uncommon in winter in lowlands. Breeds across North America to eastern Siberia, south in mountains to New Mexico. Winters both coasts, southern interior states, Mexico.

Where to Find: In summer on alpine tundra, e.g., Mount Rainier, Hurricane Ridge. Widespread in migration although uncommon in urban areas. Reliable in winter on farm fields in Snohomish, Skagit Counties.

Habitat: Breeds in high-altitude tundra; migrants, winter birds use plowed fields, meadows, dried pond margins, beaches.

Diet and Behavior: Usually walks on ground, foraging for seeds, insects. Flocks at all seasons except when nesting. Can be tame, approachable, but entire flock may flush if alarm call given.

Voice: Sharp distinctive *pi pit* call, given often in flight.

Did you know? American Pipits in breeding plumage are somewhat more lightly streaked beneath than in non-breeding plumage. Some breeding individuals may be completely unstreaked.

Date & Location Seen: _____

Juvenile

Description: 7¼". **Sleek, crested**. Silky-brown head, back grade into gray rump. Black mask, chin, **yellow belly, white undertail**. Plain-gray wings with **waxy red spots**. Blackish, square, **short tail with yellow tip**. JUVENILE: Duller with streaks below.

Similar Species: Distinctive. European Starling (page 307) has same triangular, short-tailed shape in flight, but larger with different markings.

Seasonal Abundance: Common summer resident in Region, becomes rare most winters. Returns in mid-May, almost all have moved south by November. Largest flocks appear in fall, include many juveniles. Breeds across southern Canada, northern U.S., winters south to West Indies, Panama.

Where to Find: Throughout Region, including urban areas.

Habitat: Open forest, forest edge, city parks, neighborhoods near ornamental plantings.

Diet and Behavior: Eats mostly small fruits but often flycatches during summer. Tends to flock except when nesting, descends on ripe fruit en masse. Tight, swirling flocks can number in hundreds. Calls frequently in flight, while perched.

Voice: Call high-pitched, thin *sreeee*.

Did you know? Cedar Waxwings nest late to exploit the availability of ripe fruit.

Date & Location Seen: _____

Breeding form

Gray-headed form

ORANGE-CROWNED WARBLER
Oreothlypis celata

Description: 4¾". **Plain** with obscure markings, faint, blurred breast streaks, no wing-bars, **small, pointed bill**. Best mark **vague dark line through eye**; male's dull-orange crown sometimes visible. Breeding form in Region **evenly yellow except for olive back**. Migratory northern form gray-headed, duller, **brightest yellow under tail**.

Similar Species: Yellow Warbler (page 319) very plain-faced with larger bill. Female Wilson's Warbler (page 327) shows vague dark cap, often flits tail. MacGillivray's Warbler (page 315) with more distinct hood. Warbling Vireo (page 251) gray with heavier bill.

Seasonal Abundance: Common summer resident in Region, rare in winter. Migrants return by late March; fall migration protracted, can continue into November. Breeds across Canada, south in western U.S. to Mexican border; winters Pacific Coast, southeastern U.S., Mexico south to El Salvador.

Where to Find: Breeds throughout Region, away from cities, to tree line. Migrants can be anywhere. In winter, dense, overgrown thickets, hedgerows.

Habitat: Brushy forest edge including regenerating clearcuts. Blackberry thickets preferred in winter.

Diet and Behavior: Forages relatively low on insects, some fruit. Also feeds on nectar. Joins mixed-species flocks in migration.

Voice: Song colorless trill that drops off at end. Call high, sharp chip.

Did you know? Orange-crowned Warblers sometimes feed at sapsucker wells in winter.

Date & Location Seen: _____

Male

Description: 5". Skulking warbler, **olive above** with **plain wings, gray hood, white crescents above, below eye, yellow lower breast, belly**. MALE: Hood bluish-gray. Blackish marks through eye, on bib. FEMALE: Duller with less-distinct eye crescents.

Similar Species: Gray-headed form of Orange-crowned Warbler (page 313) similar with less-distinct hood, eye crescents. Nashville Warbler (not shown; rare in Region) lacks hood, has yellow throat, complete white eye-ring.

Seasonal Abundance: Fairly common in Region, mid-April to early September. Breeds in western North America from southeastern Alaska to southwestern states, winters Mexico to Panama.

Where to Find: Locally from lowlands to near tree line. Breeders avoid urban areas. Found reliably at Snoqualmie Pass, Joint Base Lewis-McChord prairies. Migrants uncommon, secretive.

Habitat: Forest edge with dense understory, including recent clearcuts, burns, brushy Scot's-broom-dominated fields.

Diet and Behavior: Forages under cover in dense, low growth for insects. Male sometimes sings from exposed elevated perch. Pairs greet intruders with loud call notes.

Voice: Song rhythmic series of buzzy trills with last notes lower-pitched, slurred. Calls include loud, sharp *tsik*.

Did you know? MacGillivray's Warbler was first described by the early American naturalist John Townsend, who discovered it near Vancouver, Washington. John James Audubon later renamed it for Scottish naturalist William MacGillivray.

Date & Location Seen: _____

Male

Female

Description: 4¾". Wren-like warbler, olive above with **plain wings, whitish-gray belly, yellow throat, breast, undertail**. MALE: **Black "bandit" mask** bordered by white above. FEMALE: Without mask, browner.

Similar Species: Other yellowish warblers lack mask, whitish-gray belly.

Seasonal Abundance: Common resident in Region, April–September; rarely lingers into winter. Breeds across Canada, Lower 48 states, winters south to West Indies, Panama.

Where to Find: Locally throughout Region. Nisqually National Wildlife Refuge, Montlake Fill, Skagit Wildlife Area typical sites. Rare in migration away from nesting habitat.

Habitat: Low, dense, wetland vegetation, but also uses brushy, Scot's-broom-dominated fields.

Diet and Behavior: Creeps through thick cover foraging for insects. Sometimes feeds on ground. Male sings from elevated perches.

Voice: Song whistled *witchety witchety witchety witchety*. Calls include often-given *cheep*, electric-like *bizz*.

Did you know? In courtship, male Common Yellowthroats perform a flight display in which they rise up to 100 feet in the air, calling and singing.

Date & Location Seen: _____

Male

Female

Description: 4¾". Short-tailed, **all-yellow**, darker above; wings with lighter feather edges. **Dark eye prominent on plain face**. Yellow tail spots. MALE: Bright-yellow with distinct **reddish-brown breast streaks**. FEMALE: Duller, no breast streaks; can show **indistinct yellow eye-ring**.

Similar Species: Wilson's Warbler (page 327) female with longer tail, faint dark cap. Orange-crowned Warbler (page 313) with dark line through eye. Common Yellowthroat (page 317) female with gray-white belly.

Seasonal Abundance: Common resident in Region, May–September. Spring migrants continue to pass through into June; fall movement begins in July. Breeds across North America except Gulf Coast, Mojave Desert, south to South America. North American breeders winter from southern California, Mexico, West Indies to Amazonian Brazil.

Where to Find: Breeds throughout Region in appropriate habitat. Migrants more widespread.

Habitat: Near water in shrubby areas, woodland edge.

Diet and Behavior: Forages at various heights, primarily for insects, some fruit. Males feed higher in canopy than females. Joins mixed flocks in migration.

Voice: Song *sweet sweet sweet I'm so sweet*. Call notes include thin *tsip*, loud chip.

Did you know? Brown-headed Cowbirds often lay eggs in Yellow Warbler nests. To foil them, the warblers sometimes build a new nest over the top of all the eggs and lay a fresh set.

Date & Location Seen: _____

Audubon's
Male Breeding

Non-breeding

Myrtle
Male Breeding

YELLOW-RUMPED WARBLER
Setophaga coronata

Description: 5¼". **Yellow on rump**, sides of breast; **white tail spots. Brown in winter with streaked breast**. Male in breeding plumage has small yellow crown patch (sometimes obscured), gray back, **black breast with sides streaked down to white belly**. Two distinct forms in Region. MYRTLE WARBLER: **White throat**, white wing-bars, **black mask**; female browner than male, lacks bib. AUDUBON'S WARBLER: **Yellow throat**, gray head, **solid-white wing patch**; female browner than male with streaked breast, less yellow on throat. In winter, head plainer than Myrtle.

Similar Species: Distinctive in breeding plumage. In winter, separable from sparrows by thin bill, yellow rump.

Seasonal Abundance: AUDUBON'S common summer resident in Region; both forms common in migration, uncommon in winter. Breeds North America to Central America (MYRTLE in north, AUDUBON'S in West), winters south to West Indies, Panama.

Where to Find: Throughout Region.

Habitat: Breeds in coniferous forest, winters in agricultural areas, brushy woods, coastal scrub.

Diet and Behavior: Forages for insects, berries among leaves, twigs; also flycatches. Fruit intake increases in winter (wax myrtle preferred). Flocks outside breeding season.

Voice: Variable, two-part song – clear, warbled trill, usually rising or falling at end. MYRTLE chip note loud *tup*, AUDUBON'S weaker *chwit*.

Did you know? The two forms have often been considered separate species.

Date & Location Seen: _____

Male

Female Immature

Description: 4¾". **Black-and-white head pattern** with **small yellow spot in front of eye**; gray back, white wing-bars, **white underneath with dark side streaks**; white underside of tail. MALE: Black cap, cheek, extensive bib. FEMALE: Crown, cheek grayer, throat white with bib reduced (can be absent in immature).

Similar Species: Townsend's Warbler (page 325) with yellow underparts.

Seasonal Abundance: Fairly common resident in Region, mid-April to September; a few linger later. Breeds southwestern British Columbia, Colorado south to northwestern Mexico, winters southern California, Texas south through central Mexico.

Where to Find: Throughout Region at lower elevations; seldom nests in urbanized areas. Migrants widespread. Good sites include Nisqually National Wildlife Refuge, middle reaches of Snoqualmie River.

Habitat: Breeds in mature deciduous, mixed forest. Migrants use more varied habitats.

Diet and Behavior: Forages for insects at various heights in canopy. Gleans, hovers, sallies for prey. Joins mixed-species flocks in migration.

Voice: Song variable, husky series of buzz notes with emphatic ending. Calls include low, dull chip.

Did you know? In the southern portion of their breeding range Black-throated Gray Warblers are associated with oak forests – quite different from their haunts of alder and maple woods with scattered conifers in the Pacific Northwest.

Date & Location Seen: _____

Hermit Warbler

Male

Female

TOWNSEND'S WARBLER
Setophaga townsendi

Description: 4¾″. **Black-and-yellow head pattern, yellow breast with dark streaks at sides**, greenish back, white wing-bars, whitish belly. MALE: Black cap, cheek, bib, divided by bright-yellow. FEMALE: Crown, cheek lighter, bib reduced (absent in immature).

Similar Species: Black-throated Gray Warbler (page 323) lacks yellow except for dot in front of eye. **Hermit Warbler** (see inset; scarce, local in Region, breeds along coast south to California) **white below** with **yellow face, gray back**.

Seasonal Abundance: Fairly common summer resident in Region, uncommon in winter. Breeds Alaska to Idaho, winters southwestern British Columbia down coast to Mexico, Central America.

Where to Find: Throughout Region, but rarely nesting near urban areas; easier to find in intact forests at higher elevations (e.g., Mount Rainier, Snoqualmie Pass), although migrants widespread. Capitol State Forest near Olympia best bet for Hermit.

Habitat: Mature coniferous forest. Wintering birds often associate with cedars.

Diet and Behavior: Gleans, hover-gleans for insects high in canopy. Joins mixed-species flocks in migration, winter.

Voice: Buzzy song variable with several evenly-pitched notes followed by thin, high notes. Call quiet but sharp chip.

Did you know? Townsend's Warbler often hybridizes with Hermit Warbler, resulting in intermediate forms. Hybrid zones in the eastern Olympics and southwestern Cascades have resulted in the Hermit's range retreating southward.

Date & Location Seen: _____

Male

Description: 4¾". **Yellow below**, brightest on plain face, **olive-green above, wings plain**. Frequent tail-, wing-flitting. MALE: **Round inky-black cap**. FEMALE: **Indistinct cap** makes yellow eyebrow stand out. IMMATURE: Lighter cap.

Similar Species: Yellow Warbler (page 319) female with shorter tail, lacks any trace of cap. Orange-crowned Warbler (page 313) with dark line through eye, thinner bill.

Seasonal Abundance: Common resident in Region, mid-April to mid-September. Extremely rare in winter. Breeds across northern North America, south in western mountains to northern New Mexico, central California. Winters Gulf Coast, Mexico south to Panama.

Where to Find: Throughout Region, but nesting uncommon in urban areas. Common migrant in all habitats.

Habitat: Nests in moist tangles, thickets near openings in deciduous or mixed woods, including regenerating clearcuts.

Diet and Behavior: Flits through foliage at various heights feeding mostly on insects. Sallies, gleans from small branches. Eats some berries. Sings constantly in spring.

Voice: Song emphatic series of slurred chips that builds in volume, speed. Call nasal *timp*, quite different from other warblers.

Did you know? Wilson's Warbler and four other American bird species are named for pioneering ornithologist Alexander Wilson.

Date & Location Seen: _____

Male

Juvenile

Description: 7¾″. **Dark hood**, upper body contrast with **rufous sides, white belly. Bold white spots on back, white outer corners on black tail**. Dark conical bill, red eye. Male black, female grayer. JUVENILE: Heavily streaked, lacks hood.

Similar Species: Dark-eyed Junco (page 345) smaller, bill pinkish, entire tail edge white, lacks white back spots. Smaller size, lack of white tail corners separate streaked sparrows from juvenile towhee.

Seasonal Abundance: Common resident in Region except at higher elevations in winter. Ranges from southern British Columbia throughout western North America to Guatemala; northern interior birds move south in winter.

Where to Find: Throughout Region, primarily lowlands; also mountains, but absent from closed-canopy forests. Thrives in urban areas, nesting in backyards.

Habitat: Open woods with dense, shrubby understory; thickets, overgrown fields.

Diet and Behavior: Forages mostly on ground for seeds, insects, fruits. Has been recorded taking lizards, small vertebrates. Scratches ground vigorously with both feet while feeding. Does not flock, although found with other sparrows. Eats spilled grain on ground below bird feeders.

Voice: Song variable, buzzy trill. Call, given often, rising *schreeee*.

Did you know? The Spotted Towhee is quite variable throughout its large range. It and the closely-related Eastern Towhee were long treated as a single species, the Rufous-sided Towhee.

Date & Location Seen: _____

Breeding

Juvenile

Description: 5¼". **Slim,** fairly long-tailed sparrow with streaked back, **unstreaked gray breast.** BREEDING: **Rufous cap bordered by white eyebrow,** black line through eye. NON-BREEDING: Browner; cap dull, streaked. JUVENILE: Resembles non-breeding but with streaked breast, pinkish bill.

Similar Species: Other small sparrows in Region shorter-tailed, less slim-appearing. American Tree Sparrow (not shown; rare winter resident in Region) similar but with central breast spot, less-distinct rufous eye-line.

Seasonal Abundance: Fairly common but very local summer resident in Region (much more common in dry forests of eastern Washington). Breeds across continent from central Alaska, Newfoundland, south through U.S., in mountains to Nicaragua. Winters southern U.S., Mexico southward through breeding range.

Where to Find: Mostly drier places, including South Sound Prairies, San Juan Islands; also near mountain passes.

Habitat: Open woods, woodland edge with grassy areas.

Diet and Behavior: Forages mostly on ground for seeds, insects. Seldom observed in flocks in Region. Sometimes sallies for flying insects.

Voice: Song mechanical-sounding long trill, all on one pitch. Calls include sharp chip, thin *seet*.

Did you know? Chipping Sparrows make use of animal hair in building their nests. Woven hair makes up the bulk of the nest in some cases.

Date & Location Seen: _____

Description: 5¹/₄″. **Small, streaked below**, above. **Short notched tail**, whitish central crown stripe, **yellowish eyebrow**, pinkish bill, legs. Eyebrow yellower in spring, summer.

Similar Species: Song Sparrow (page 337) larger; richer brown with dense, thick streaks on breast. Lincoln's Sparrow (page 339) gray-headed with buff mustache mark, finer breast streaks. Vesper Sparrow (not shown; rare summer resident of remnant lowland prairies in Region) has longer, white-edged tail.

Seasonal Abundance: Common summer resident in Region, rare in winter.

Where to Find: Grasslands throughout Region in summer. A few may linger in winter in open areas of Snohomish, King Counties. Migrants occur out of habitat near open spaces, even in cities.

Habitat: Open grassland, agricultural fields, salt marsh, associated edges.

Diet and Behavior: Forages mostly on ground for insects, seeds. Forms flocks, especially in migration, winter. Male sings from elevated perches.

Voice: Buzzy song of 2–3 longer notes followed by lower-pitched, less-clear buzzes. Calls include sharp, high, but quiet *pik*, thin *tsew*.

Did you know? The song of the Savannah Sparrow varies from place to place, even within the Puget Sound Region.

Date & Location Seen: _____

Sooty

Slate-colored

Description: 6¼". Bulky, **plain-faced sparrow with chevron-shaped spots** on whitish breast, reddish-brown tail, yellowish lower bill. Two distinct forms in Region. SOOTY: Variably **dark-chocolate-brown** to gray-brown with **dense markings below**. SLATE-COLORED: **Gray on head, back** contrasting with rusty wings.

Similar Species: Song Sparrow (page 337) has gray eyebrow. Hermit Thrush (page 301) has thin bill.

Seasonal Abundance: SOOTY: Common migrant, winter resident in Region, early September–early May; scarce breeder on a few San Juan Islands. Coastal; breeds Alaska to Washington, winters to California. SLATE-COLORED: Fairly common summer resident in Region in Cascades near subalpine zone; rare in lowlands. Breeds mountains of northwestern North America, winters south to California.

Where to Find: SOOTY: Throughout Region at lower elevations. SLATE-COLORED: Snoqualmie, Stevens Passes most accessible sites.

Habitat: In lowlands, brushy fields, forest edge including backyards; blackberry thickets, dense tangles preferred. Mountain breeding habitat meadow edges near small trees.

Diet and Behavior: Forages mostly on ground for seeds, insects, some fruit. Scrapes ground with both feet, jumping forward, kicking back. Sings fall, spring in lowlands. Visits feeders.

Voice: Song rich, complex, melodic, staccato, lively. Calls include hard, smacking *chink*.

Did you know? Highly variable across its continent-wide range, Fox Sparrow is often treated as four separate species.

Date & Location Seen: _____

Description: 6". Streaked brownish above with brown wings. **Dark, dense streaking** may merge into central spot on whitish breast. **Long, rounded tail pumped in flight. Wide gray eyebrow**, brown crown with gray central stripe, dark mustache mark. JUVENILE: Buffy below.

Similar Species: Fox Sparrow (page 335) lacks broad eyebrow. Savannah (page 333), Lincoln's (page 339) Sparrows more trim-appearing. Swamp Sparrow (not shown; rare winter resident in Region) plain-gray below.

Seasonal Abundance: Common resident in Region. Ranges across North America, south to northern Mexico.

Where to Find: Most abundant sparrow in Region; found throughout, up to mountain passes.

Habitat: Prefers shrubs, thicket edge in wetter areas, but frequents all semi-open habitats, broken forest.

Diet and Behavior: Feeds mostly on ground on insects, seeds (including below bird feeders), some fruit. Less prone to flock but can be gregarious in migration. Sings year round; in Region, begins nesting in late winter.

Voice: Song begins with several clear notes followed by lower note, jumbled trill. Calls include distinctive nasal *chump*, thin *seet*.

Did you know? Over 30 subspecies of this highly variable sparrow have been recognized. Song Sparrows resident in the Puget Sound Region are among the darkest. In migration and winter they are joined by other races, including a few lighter-colored birds.

Date & Location Seen: _____

Description: 5¼". **Small**, secretive. Streaked above, below. **Buff wash on breast with distinct fine, dark streaks that end abruptly** at clear-white belly. Short tail, small bill, grayish face with divided brown crown, **buff mustache mark**, faint eye-ring.

Similar Species: Smaller than Song Sparrow (page 337), with finer streaks. Lacks white or yellow eyebrow of Savannah Sparrow (page 333).

Seasonal Abundance: Common migrant, fairly common in winter at lower elevations in Region. Fairly common breeder in Cascades, May–September. Breeds from Alaska across Canada, south in western mountains; winters U.S. coasts, West Indies, south through Middle America.

Where to Find: Widespread in lowlands in winter, scarce in developed areas. In summer, around Stevens, Snoqualmie Passes, higher elevations of North Cascades Highway.

Habitat: Breeds in open meadows, bogs. Prefers wet, scrubby places at all seasons, but migrants use variety of habitats.

Diet and Behavior: Feeds mostly on ground on seeds, insects, in or near cover. Less often in groups, but flocks with other sparrows.

Voice: Song fairly long series of bubbly musical trills, notes, generally given only on nesting grounds. Call sharp but soft chip.

Did you know? In fall, Lincoln's Sparrows often associate with other sparrows in wet fields; in spring, they may keep company with warblers in drier sites.

Date & Location Seen: _____

Breeding

White-throated Sparrow

Immature

Description: 6½″. Fairly large, long-tailed, with **unstreaked gray breast, black-and-white head stripes, yellowish-orange bill**. Faint white wing-bars, streaked back. IMMATURE: **Brown-and-gray head stripes**. JUVENILE: Streaked breast in summer.

Similar Species: **White-throated Sparrow** (see inset; uncommon in Region in winter) browner, smaller, with **clearly-marked, bright-white throat**. Golden-crowned Sparrow (page 343) has dusky bill, immature with less-defined head stripes.

Seasonal Abundance: Common summer resident in Region, less common in winter. Breeds across northern North America, south to California in West; winters Pacific Coast, western, central U.S., to Caribbean, Mexico.

Where to Find: Nests throughout Region up to mountain passes, including cities. Winters locally in lowlands, mostly in agricultural areas.

Habitat: Shrubby woodland edge, parks, cities. Farms, hedgerows preferred in winter.

Diet and Behavior: Forages mostly on ground for insects, seeds, other plant material. Occasionally flycatches from trees, bushes. Flocks with other sparrows.

Voice: Song begins with 1–2 whistled calls followed by rhythmic series of buzzy trilled notes. Calls include sharp *bink*, high, thin *seet*.

Did you know? Puget White-crowned Sparrow – the subspecies that nests in western Washington – winters mostly in California. Some remain for the winter in the Puget Sound Region, joined by larger numbers of Gambel's White-crowned Sparrow, which breeds farther north.

Date & Location Seen: _____

Breeding

Immature

Description: 6¾". **Large, with unstreaked gray breast**, long tail, relatively small **dusky bill**. Streaked brown above with **two white wing-bars**. BREEDING: **Golden crown bordered by black cap**. NON-BREEDING: Lacks black, has only hint of gold. IMMATURE: Resembles non-breeding.

Similar Species: White-crowned Sparrow (page 341) appears grayer, with orange-pink bill; adult has black-and-white head stripes (brown-and-buff in immature).

Seasonal Abundance: Common winter resident in Region. Arrives mid-September, departs by mid-May. Breeds from Alaska south through British Columbia to U.S. border. Winters along coast from just north of Washington to northern Baja California.

Where to Find: In winter, lower elevations throughout Region. Migrants also at high elevations.

Habitat: Brushy places, including neighborhoods.

Diet and Behavior: Forages on ground for seeds, insects, often in flocks with other sparrows. Also feeds in trees, shrubs on blossoms, buds, especially in spring. Occasionally flycatches from trees, bushes.

Voice: Song, often given in migration, series of several long, raspy, whistled notes. Call notes include thin *seep*, rich, loud *bink*.

Did you know? Golden-crowned Sparrows wander regularly as far as the East Coast.

Date & Location Seen: _____

Oregon
Male

Oregon
Female

Slate-colored

Oregon
Juvenile

Description: 5¾". Sparrow-shaped. Short **pink conical bill, white outer tail feathers**, whitish belly. Two distinct forms in Region. OREGON JUNCO: Male with **black hood**, plain-brown back; female duller with gray hood. SLATE-COLORED JUNCO: Completely **grayish** with white belly.

Similar Species: Vesper Sparrow (not shown; rare in Region) streaked above, below, lacks hood; other sparrows in Region lack white outer tail feathers. Juvenile juncos streaked above, below, can be mistaken for sparrow but have white tail edges, pinkish bill.

Seasonal Abundance: Common resident in Region; numbers increase in lowlands in winter. OREGON: Common year round (breeds, winters in West); SLATE-COLORED: Small numbers appear in winter (breeds northern forests, winters throughout Lower 48 states).

Where to Find: Throughout Region; nests uncommonly in suburban areas.

Habitat: Nests in coniferous, mixed woods, particularly at brushy edges. In migration, winter can appear anywhere, including cities.

Diet and Behavior: Flocks forage on ground, also in trees, mostly for seeds, insects. Often scratches at ground with feet. Regular beneath bird feeders.

Voice: Trilled song similar to that of Chipping Sparrow but more musical. Most common call sharp *tsip*.

Did you know? Oregon and Slate-colored are just two of the many distinctive regional forms of the widely distributed, highly variable Dark-eyed Junco.

Date & Location Seen: _____

Male Breeding

Female

Description: 6¾". Compact, with **fairly stout bill**. MALE: Black back, tail, wings, **yellow-and-white wing-bars**. Adult **bright yellow with scarlet head** in breeding plumage; immature, non-breeding-plumaged birds lack red on head. FEMALE: Lacks red head. Olive replaces black areas of male; back, belly can be gray. Wing-bars reduced but still conspicuous.

Similar Species: Bullock's Oriole (page 359) with much more pointed bill, orange tail. Warblers smaller.

Seasonal Abundance: Common resident in Region, May–early September; uncommon into October. Breeds in West from northwestern Canada to Mexican border, winters Mexico to Costa Rica.

Where to Find: Throughout Region, but rarely nests successfully in urban areas. Easiest to spot at forest edges. Migrants can be inconspicuous in canopy.

Habitat: Fairly open coniferous or mixed forest; migrants use varied habitats.

Diet and Behavior: Gleans methodically in treetops, mostly for insects; occasionally sallies. Also takes fruit, especially in fall. Migrants often move in small flocks.

Voice: Song short series of slow phrases similar to that of American Robin, but hoarser. Call distinctive *pid er ick*.

Did you know? Recent research has confirmed that Western Tanager is not a member of the tanager family, but instead belongs to a family of finch-like birds that includes Black-headed Grosbeak (page 349) and Lazuli Bunting (page 297).

Date & Location Seen: _____

Male

Female

BLACK-HEADED GROSBEAK
Pheucticus melanocephalus

Description: 7¾". Larger than most finches. **Plump**, square-tailed, with **large conical bill**. MALE: Adult with black head, tail, wings. **Wings, tail with bold white marks**. Breast, rump tawny-brown. Immature without black head. FEMALE: Brown with little white in wings, tail. Strong **white head stripe, eyebrow, mustache mark**.

Similar Species: Evening Grosbeak (page 371) male with yellow eyebrow, female with plain head.

Seasonal Abundance: Common summer resident in Region. Migrants (often seen in cities) arrive in May, first fall transients late July. Breeds in West, from southern British Columbia south through mountains of Mexico; winters Mexico.

Where to Find: Throughout Region up to mountain passes.

Habitat: Nests mostly in mature deciduous or mixed forests away from urban areas, but in migration more widespread.

Diet and Behavior: Insects, seeds, berries. Forages in trees. Occasional at bird feeders.

Voice: Melodious song long, whistled warble likened to "drunken robin". Distinctive call note, sharp *pik*, often reveals its presence.

Did you know? Both the male and the female Black-headed Grosbeak sing, which is not uncommon among finch-like birds.

Date & Location Seen: _____

Male

Female

RED-WINGED BLACKBIRD
Agelaius phoeniceus

Description: 8¾". Medium-sized blackbird with fairly **stout, pointed bill**. MALE: **Glossy-black with red shoulder patch** bordered with yellow-buff. FEMALE: Smaller; dark-brown above, **heavily streaked** below with strong **buff eyebrow**.

Similar Species: Other blackbirds lack shoulder patch. Sparrows smaller than female Red-winged Blackbird, with more conical bill.

Seasonal Abundance: Common resident in Region. In winter shifts from marshes to farms, retreats from higher altitudes. Breeds across continent south of subarctic zone to Bahamas, Central America; leaves northern areas in winter.

Where to Find: Nests throughout Region up to mountain passes in suitable habitat. In winter roosts in wetlands but feeds more in agricultural areas.

Habitat: Marshes, meadows, brushy edge. Farms, feedlots in winter.

Diet and Behavior: Seeds, insects. Forages mostly on ground but sometimes in trees. Flocks with other blackbirds. Often at bird feeders. During nesting, polygamous males protect their territory with frequent song, aggressively chasing out all intruders.

Voice: Main song of male *conk a ree*. Calls include *chek* note, rattles.

Did you know? Red-winged Blackbirds give more than 20 different vocalizations, a reflection of their complex social organization. Males have 18 different calls, females six. Four alarm calls are given by both sexes.

Date & Location Seen: _____

Description: 9″. Heavy-bodied, **short-tailed** member of blackbird family. Back, sides streaked brown. **Bright-yellow underparts** with V-shaped black breast band. **Outer tail feathers white**. In flight, weak flapping alternates with gliding.

Similar Species: European Starling (page 307) lacks yellow underparts, white outer tail feathers.

Seasonal Abundance: Rare summer resident in Region, uncommon in winter. Breeds from southern British Columbia to Michigan, south through Mexican highlands; winters from all but northernmost part of breeding range south to Gulf states, Mexico.

Where to Find: Mostly gone as breeder in Region; still nests in prairies near Fort Lewis. Winters throughout Region in low-elevation meadows, agricultural areas. Reliable sites include Skagit, Snohomish, Samish River valleys.

Habitat: Fields, prairies, farms. Frequents wet coastal habitats in winter.

Diet and Behavior: Feeds on ground for insects, seeds. Probes soil with long, pointed bill. In winter usually in flocks. Often perches, sings high in trees, even during migration, winter; also sings from ground.

Voice: Song gurgling series of flute-like notes. Calls include *chupp*, rattle; thin, high buzz in flight.

Did you know? The Western Meadowlark is visually almost identical to the Eastern Meadowlark. Noting its different song, John James Audubon recognized that Western Meadowlark was a different species. He named it *neglecta* in Latin because others had overlooked it.

Date & Location Seen: _____

Male

Female

Description: 9″. Medium-sized blackbird with **short, pointed bill**, fairly long, rounded tail. MALE: **Glossy blackish-green with purplish-iridescent head, light-yellow eye**. FEMALE: **Drab** gray-brown with dark eye.

Similar Species: Red-winged Blackbird (page 351) not as plain; female streaked, male with shoulder patch. Brown-headed Cowbird (page 357) smaller, bill more finch-like.

Seasonal Abundance: Common resident in Region, but local. Breeds across much of West, upper Midwest, south to California; winters in warmer parts of breeding range, southern Great Plains, western Gulf Coast states, Mexico.

Where to Find: Patchily distributed around cities; much easier to find in agricultural areas.

Habitat: Pastures, feed lots, urban parking lots, other open places.

Diet and Behavior: Mostly insects, seeds; also waste grain, crumbs. Forages mostly on ground, often in flocks – sometimes with other blackbirds, starlings. Visits bird feeders.

Voice: Courting male has *kseee* call. Year-round nasal *check* note.

Did you know? Nest-site selection by Brewer's Blackbirds varies greatly depending on local availability. They may build their nests in trees, on plant stalks over water, in low shrubs, on the ground in high grass, or even on rocky ledges.

Date & Location Seen: _____

Male

Female

Juvenile

Description: 7½". Small blackbird with **stubby conical bill**, relatively **short, square-tipped tail**. MALE: Black with **brown head**. FEMALE: Smaller, **plain** gray-brown, lighter below, with vague streaks. JUVENILE: Similar to female but paler, streaking more distinct.

Similar Species: Short bill, brown head distinguish male from other blackbirds. Female smaller than blackbirds, plainer than sparrows.

Seasonal Abundance: Common summer resident in Region, most depart in winter. Breeds across North America from southern Yukon, Newfoundland, south through central Mexico; winters Midwest, southern states, Mexico.

Where to Find: Throughout Region, including cities.

Habitat: Widespread in breeding season in woodlands, neighborhoods, open areas. In migration prefers fields, farms.

Diet and Behavior: Feeds on ground, mostly on seeds, insects. Does not build nest, instead lays eggs in other birds' nests. In breeding season groups of males display with odd postures, spread wings, noisily chase females. Flocks with other blackbirds after breeding.

Voice: Male gives gurgling squeaks in display. Female rattles. Flight call thin, high whistle. Juvenile begs from host species with *cheep*, given frequently.

Did you know? Brown-headed Cowbirds, once restricted to plains habitats, invaded more-forested regions as land was cleared for agriculture, settlement, and lumber production. Cowbird nest parasitism is now implicated in the decline of many forest songbirds.

Date & Location Seen: _____

357

Male

Male Immature

Female

Description: 8″. **Slim** with long tail, **tapered, pointed bill**. ADULT: Male **orange** with black cap, back, wings, eye-line, narrow bib, center of tail. **Large white wing patch**. Female duller, mostly gray-olive with whitish belly, **white wing-bars, orange wash on head, throat**. IMMATURE: Like female; male brighter with black throat.

Similar Species: Male unmistakable in Region. Size, bill shape distinguish female from warblers, grosbeaks.

Seasonal Abundance: Uncommon summer resident in Region. Arrives May, most depart by early August. Breeds southwestern Canada to Mexico, winters Mexico, Guatemala.

Where to Find: Mostly limited to low-elevation river edge, but also open groves, parks, suburban neighborhoods. Good bets include Skagit, Snoqualmie, Stillaguamish Rivers.

Habitat: Prefers deciduous or mixed woodlands with large shade trees, especially cottonwoods along rivers.

Diet and Behavior: Forages in foliage of trees, bushes for insects, fruits, nectar from flowers. Weaves hanging bag-shaped nest in outer limbs, concealed by leaves but obvious in winter. Sometimes visits hummingbird feeders.

Voice: Series of rich, medium-pitched whistles, chatter. Calls include harsh *cshek*, rolling chatter.

Did you know? New World orioles such as Bullock's are not orioles at all, but blackbirds – a New World family. Early naturalists gave them that name because they superficially resemble the Golden Oriole of Europe, a member of an unrelated Old World family.

Date & Location Seen: _____

Male

Female

PURPLE FINCH
Haemorhous purpureus

Description: 5¾″. Stocky finch with **short, notched tail, stout bill**. MALE: **Raspberry-red** on head, breast, extending to flanks, infusing brown back. Adult **without streaks on belly**. FEMALE: Brownish without red. Blurry streaks on whitish-buff breast, belly. **Broad white eyebrow**.

Similar Species: House Finch (page 363) slimmer, male more orange-red with streaks on belly. Female lacks broad white eyebrow.

Seasonal Abundance: Locally fairly common resident, migrant in Region. Transients appear in urbanized areas late April–early May. Breeds across continent in northern forests, south in Appalachians, Pacific coastal mountains. Winters eastern U.S., Pacific Coast states to Baja California.

Where to Find: Throughout rural, semi-rural parts of Region, e.g., Snoqualmie Valley, Skagit Wildlife Area, Kitsap Peninsula. Uncommon in cites, avoids dense forests.

Habitat: Mixed woods, coniferous forest edge, semi-open areas with fruiting trees.

Diet and Behavior: Forages on fruits, seeds, buds, some insects, mostly in flocks, especially outside nesting season. More arboreal than House Finch, but also feeds on ground. Uses bird feeders.

Voice: Series of warbled notes without harsh ending of House Finch song. Calls include muffled whistle, sharp *pik* given in flight.

Did you know? Purple Finches have undergone serious decline in urbanized Puget Sound, often attributed to competition with the recently-arrived and more adaptable House Finch. Other factors may also be involved.

Date & Location Seen: _____

Male

Female

Description: 5¹⁄₂″. Sparrow-sized finch with long, only slightly notched tail. **Bill short, rounded**. MALE: Red (yellow in some individuals) on crown, breast, rump; **streaks on belly, flanks**. FEMALE: Brownish-gray without red. Blurry streaks on gray-white breast, belly. **No strong facial pattern**.

Similar Species: Purple Finch (page 361) more robust, adult male without streaks on lower breast, female with broad white eyebrow.

Seasonal Abundance: Common year-round resident in Region. Ranges from southern Canada south through Mexico.

Where to Find: Throughout Region, including cities, up to mountain passes.

Habitat: Urban neighborhoods, parks, suburbs, farms, woodland edge. Avoids dense forest.

Diet and Behavior: Often nests, feeds in backyards. Usually forages in flocks on ground, in weeds, or in trees for seeds, berries, blossoms, buds. Regular at sunflower feeders.

Voice: Series of cheery warbling notes often ending with harsh note. Call loud chirp.

Did you know? Native to deserts, scrublands, grasslands, and open forests of Mexico and the American West, House Finches extended their range as land was cleared for human settlement, first reaching the Puget Sound Region in the 1950s. House Finches introduced to New York City in the 1940s have now spread throughout eastern North America.

Date & Location Seen: _____

Female

Male

Description: 6″. Compact finch with **large head, short, notched tail**, plain, dark wings. **Bill heavy with crossed tips**. MALE: Plumage variable; generally brick-red, sometimes orange, yellowish – brightest on crown, rump. FEMALE: Olive-yellow. JUVENILE: Dull, streaked.

Similar Species: Purple Finch (page 361), House Finch (page 363) smaller, less stubby, without crossed bill tips. Pine Grosbeak (not shown; rare in Region) larger with white wing-bars, uncrossed bill. White-winged Crossbill (not shown; rare in Region) with white wing-bars.

Seasonal Abundance: Fairly common resident in Region. Nests at any time of year. Movements occur through cities, generally April–May. Ranges world wide, mostly above equator.

Where to Find: Erratic, nomadic. Localities, abundance vary with cone crops.

Habitat: Coniferous forest, including pine, spruce, Douglas-fir. Also mixed woods.

Diet and Behavior: Flocks seek productive conifers, pry cones open, extract seeds. Also eats buds, other seeds, insects, minerals from ground. Occasional at bird feeders.

Voice: Song rapid series of hard chirps, warbles. *Kip kip* call given in flight.

Did you know? There are at least eight different forms of Red Crossbill in North America, varying in bill size and in subtleties of their call notes. Each may wander in search of the cone type that its bill is best adapted to open.

Date & Location Seen: _____

Description: 4³/₄″. Upperparts streaked brownish, underparts buff-white with **well-defined, heavy, dark streaking**. Yellowish on wings, tail, not always visible on perched bird, but male's bold yellow wing stripe evident in flight. Tail notched. **Bill conical, long, pointed**.

Similar Species: Smaller than House Finch (page 363), Purple Finch (page 361); bill shape distinguishes from warblers, other finches. Common Redpoll (not shown; rare winter visitor in Region) has black chin, red cap.

Seasonal Abundance: Common resident in Region but can be scarce, local in late summer, fall. Breeds from Alaska across Canada, south through western U.S. to Guatemala; winters in all but northernmost part of breeding range, throughout U.S., Mexico.

Where to Find: Widespread in Region, usually near conifers. Migratory, nomadic; local abundance varies unpredictably.

Habitat: Coniferous forest, mixed woods (especially with alders), weedy areas.

Diet and Behavior: Gregarious. Feeds mostly in trees, but also on weed stalks, ground. Eats mostly seeds, but some insects taken. Large, compact flocks swirl noisily when alarmed. Flocks with other finches. Regular at thistle, black-oil sunflower feeders.

Voice: Song jumble of husky twitters, trills. Calls include rising *zreeee*, high, sharp *di di di*, both given in flight.

Did you know? In spring, Pine Siskins often glean insects from large limbs, feeding somewhat like a nuthatch.

Date & Location Seen: _____

Male Breeding

Female Breeding

Juvenile

Description: 5". Variable plumage with **prominent wing-bars**, white undertail. **Short, conical bill**, pinkish in summer. BREEDING: Male **bright-yellow** with black wings, forehead, tail. Female dull-yellow, olive on back, with **blackish wings**. NON-BREEDING: Dull with some yellow on throat. JUVENILE: Browner on back with buff wing-bars.

Similar Species: Conical bill distinguishes from warblers; lack of streaks from sparrows, other finches.

Seasonal Abundance: Fairly common resident in Region. Migratory; often difficult to find in winter. Breeds from southern Canada south to California, Oklahoma, Georgia; winters in all but northern fringe of breeding area, south through U.S. to Mexico.

Where to Find: Throughout Region; less common in cities but frequents neighborhoods, weedy lots.

Habitat: Weedy, open areas with some deciduous trees; farms, openings in forest.

Diet and Behavior: Gregarious. Flocks most evident late summer, fall. Late nesting coincides with summer seed production. Eats small seeds on weed stalks, especially thistles (favors thistle feeders in backyards), also in trees such as alder, birch, sometimes on ground.

Voice: Song long jumble of high, repeated twitters, phrases. Calls include *tee di di di*, mostly given in flight, thin *twee*.

Did you know? The American Goldfinch is the state bird of Washington, and also of Iowa and New Jersey.

Date & Location Seen: _____

Male

Female

EVENING GROSBEAK
Coccothraustes vespertinus

Description: 8″. Plump, short-tailed finch with **massive conical bill**. Black wings, tail with **large white patches** on each. Bill green in spring, whitish in winter. MALE: **Bright-yellow eyebrow**. Dusky-brown head, chest grade to yellow belly, back. FEMALE: Brownish-gray with yellowish wash.

Similar Species: Black-headed Grosbeak (page 349) lacks yellow eyebrow of male, plain head of female. American Goldfinch (page 369) much smaller.

Seasonal Abundance: Fairly common in Region in summer, less common, irregular in winter. Easiest to find in May, even in cities. Ranges across southern Canada, south in western mountains to Mexico; some southward movement in winter.

Where to Find: Widespread but local, mostly near coniferous woods. Less common nesting at low elevations.

Habitat: Primarily coniferous forest but also mixed woods.

Diet and Behavior: Gregarious outside breeding season. Large flocks may forage together, mostly in trees, on seeds, buds including maple, ash. Also eats insects, fruit, comes to ground for gravel. Regular at bird feeders (usually voracious).

Voice: Song repeated notes in series. Call strident, ringing *tcheew* given often by flocking birds.

Did you know? Their scientific and common names come from the erroneous notion that Evening Grosbeaks are most active after sunset, dating back to the first scientific description of the species in 1825.

Date & Location Seen: _____

Male

Female

Description: 6″. An Old World sparrow, not closely related to native sparrows. **Chunky**, short-tailed, with **unstreaked** dingy-gray breast, brown-streaked upperparts. MALE: Gray crown, **black face, bib**, with chestnut hind neck. Colors duller in winter. FEMALE: Plain, dull, with **light-buff eyebrow**.

Similar Species: Native sparrows not as compact. Finches of similar size streaked.

Seasonal Abundance: Common resident in Region. Introduced from Europe to North America, most of world.

Where to Find: Throughout Region, usually near human habitation.

Habitat: Cities, suburbs, farms.

Diet and Behavior: Feeds on ground, often in flocks, mostly on seeds, insects, crumbs. Noisily roosts in thick bushes. Competes aggressively for cavity nest sites, much to detriment of native species. Regular at bird feeders.

Voice: Repeated series of *chirrup* notes. Chirping call often given by many birds simultaneously, creating cheerful din. Also rattles in excitement.

Did you know? Male House Sparrows get brighter as they begin nesting, not as a result of molting, but through feather wear that reveals the attractive colors beneath.

Date & Location Seen: _____

White-tailed Ptarmigan

Sooty Grouse

Northern Goshawk
Adult

Northern Goshawk
Immature

WHITE-TAILED PTARMIGAN
Lagopus leucura

Chicken-like bird of alpine meadows. In summer, protectively colored in brown, black, buffy; tail white-edged. Male (shown) has white belly, bare red skin (sometimes concealed) above eye. In Region, fairly common but furtive resident of high Cascades; sits quietly, blends into background when intruders present. Winter birds pure-white but seldom seen because habitat inaccessible then.

SOOTY GROUSE
Dendragapus fuliginosus

Large chicken-like bird of conifer forests. Tail with gray band at tip. Male (shown) upperparts mostly sooty-brown, underparts bluish-gray; female lighter, bluish tones muted. Now absent from most of lowlands in Region due to deforestation, but fairly common from foothills to mountain passes. Often detected by male's call, series of soft, low, far-carrying hoots, from perch high in tree.

NORTHERN GOSHAWK
Accipiter gentilis

Large, heavy-bodied, long-tailed forest hawk. Glides between short bursts of flapping. ADULT: Dark-gray above, light-gray beneath, with black cap, white eyebrow, black eye-line. IMMATURE: Larger version of Cooper's Hawk (page 119), heavily-streaked beneath to undertail; bands on broad tail form wavy pattern when bird perched. Uncommon resident of older forest at higher elevations in Region; rare winter visitor in lowlands.

American Three-toed Woodpecker

Gray Jay

Clark's Nutcracker

AMERICAN THREE-TOED WOODPECKER
Picoides dorsalis

Black-and-white woodpecker of subalpine forests. Compare Hairy Woodpecker (page 227). White back, flanks, barred with black. White mustache mark, line behind eye. Male (shown) has yellow crown patch. Uncommon resident in Region near Cascade crest; easily overlooked except when busily engaged in flaking bark from trees. Often concentrates in recently-burned areas to exploit insect infestations in standing charred timber.

GRAY JAY
Perisoreus canadensis

Distinctive, small-billed jay of conifer forests. Adult (shown) has dark-gray upperparts, light-gray underparts. Dark cap set off by light forehead, cheeks. Juvenile overall dark-gray. Curious; begs from tourists, steals food in campgrounds. Often roams in family groups. Fairly common in intact, mid- to high-elevation conifer forest throughout Region. Rare in lowlands.

CLARK'S NUTCRACKER
Nucifraga columbiana

Distinctive relative of crows, jays, specialized for extracting seeds from pine cones. Medium-gray with long, black, pointed bill. Wings black with white patch on inner trailing edge conspicuous in flight. Tail black with white edges. In Region, fairly common but local resident at higher elevations of Cascades, uncommon in Olympics. Pesters tourists, campers for handouts.

Horned Lark

Mountain Chickadee

Mountain Bluebird
Male

Mountain Bluebird
Female

HORNED LARK
Eremophila alpestris

Small songbird of short-grass habitats. Male streaked grayish-brown above, plain-white below, with black breast band, mask, white eyebrow. Small, dark "horns" protrude from crown behind eye. Female (shown) paler, lacks horns. Fairly common summer resident of alpine meadows in Region, rare in winter in lowlands. Widespread, highly variable species; individuals of other populations yellower on head, breast, sometimes found in lowlands, rarely nesting.

MOUNTAIN CHICKADEE
Poecile gambeli

Chickadee of dry, open forests. Very similar to Black-capped Chickadee (page 273) but with white eyebrow; wing feathers lack white edging. *Chick a dee* call hoarser, slower. Fairly common resident in Region in subalpine zone on rain-shadowed east side of Mount Rainier (Sunrise), locally elsewhere along Cascade crest. Very rare visitor to lowland feeders in winter.

MOUNTAIN BLUEBIRD
Sialia currucoides

Bluebird of dry, open country, parklands. MALE: All-blue, unmistakable in Region. FEMALE: Similar to Western Bluebird (page 297) but more slender with thinner bill, longer wings, tail; breast usually grayer but can be pale-orangish. In Region, fairly common summer resident in subalpine zone on rain-shadowed east side of Mount Rainier (Sunrise), locally elsewhere along Cascade crest. Rare but regular migrant through lowlands, especially spring.

Townsend's Solitaire

Gray-crowned Rosy-Finch

Cassin's Finch Male

Cassin's Finch Female

TOWNSEND'S SOLITAIRE
Myadestes townsendi

Ground-nesting thrush of higher-elevation forests. Slender, short-billed. Overall gray with prominent white eye-ring, white tail edges. Buffy wing stripe visible in flight, shows as small patch on folded wing. Fairly common but local summer resident in Region in open forests, parklands of high Cascades, Olympics. In lowlands, uncommon spring migrant (especially in San Juans, Cascade foothills), rare fall migrant, winter resident.

GRAY-CROWNED ROSY-FINCH
Leucosticte tephrocotis

Chunky finch of high-mountain tundra. Bill fairly short, conical. Legs, feet black; bill yellow in winter, black in breeding season. Male (shown) mostly rich-brown with pinkish tones on belly, rump, wings. Throat, forehead dark, rest of head gray. Female, juvenile duller. Fairly common breeder in remote, rocky clefts at edge of snowfields on alpine meadows in Region; easier to find in late summer when flocking. Rare visitor to lowlands in migration, winter.

CASSIN'S FINCH
Haemorhous cassinii

Dry-forest counterpart of very similar Purple Finch (page 361). MALE: Slightly crested; crown brighter red than rest of head. Back less red than Purple Finch; lower belly lightly streaked. FEMALE: Underparts more finely streaked than Purple Finch; white eyebrow indistinct. Flight call *kitty up*. Reaches Region locally along Cascade crest; fairly common summer resident in subalpine zone on rain-shadowed east side of Mount Rainier (Sunrise).

Acknowledgments, Photographer Credits

Creating a bird identification guide is a significant undertaking and would not be possible without the contribution of many local birders. Don Kraege, Kelly McAllister, Dennis Paulson, Russell Rogers, Patricia Thompson, and Bill Tweit generously shared their expertise on birds of the Puget Sound Region. Our classification scheme for Regional habitats is adapted with the authors' permission from *A Guide to Bird Finding in Washington* by Terry Wahl and Dennis Paulson (first published 1971, now out of print). We acknowledge the very capable technical review and editorial comments by Steve Mlodinow and Jon Dunn. Thanks to Shawn K. Morse for the Puget Sound Region map and to Eric Kraig for the bird drawings. Invaluable suggestions for the book were offered by Shannon Brady, Carlene Hughes, Sheila McCartan, Ruth Pagel, and Kristin Stewart.

We owe a great debt to the many photographers who have contributed to this book, consistently meeting the challenge of capturing a bird's key field marks in photographs of high technical and artistic merit. Their names are listed below. In particular, Tom Eckert, Dick McNeely, Jim Pruske, Robert Royse, and Brian Small spent countless hours going through their slide collections searching for just the right images for us. Special thanks are due to William Zittrich for permission to use his photo of a Rufous Hummingbird on the cover.

The letters following the page numbers refer to the position of the photograph on that page (T = top, B = bottom, L = left, R = right, N = inset).

Don Baccus: 100T, 102. **Lee Barnes**: 42B, 50B, 54T, 70B, 80, 110, 228, 124, 138TL, 184T, 198, 202, 208B, 268T, 280, 318T, 376TL, 378TR. **Tony Beck/VIREO**: 214B. **Brian Bell**: 26T, B, 30B, 64B, 180N, 216. **Rick and Nora Bowers**: 52T, 92N, 102N, 118T, 154TL, 176T, 186B, 236, 252, 320T. **Keith Brady**: 26N, 86B, 108, 132, 166, 172B, 194, 262B, 274, 330T, 356BL, 360T, B, 370T, B, 376B. **Dick Cannings**: 302B. **Jane Cooper**: 112TR. **Mike**

Danzenbaker: 182N. **Richard Day/VIREO**: 380BL. **Mike Donahue**: 122N, 168T, B. **Mike Dossett**: 190T. **Tom Eckert**: 78T, B, 116N, 144B, 148BR, 234, 238, 268B, 276T, 288, 302T, 324T, B, 334, 368N, 376TR. **James R. Gallagher/Sea & Sage Audubon**: 364. **Don Graham**: 68TR. **Carrie Griffis**: 364N. **Ralph Hocken**: 46T. **Gloria Hopkins**: 224. **Peter LaTourrette/VIREO**: 296N, 330B. **Kevin Li**: 260T, B. **Jerry Liguori**: 228N, 128T, 176B, 380TL. **Dan Logen**: 172T, 218L, R, 296T, B, 368T. **Gary Luhm**: 38T, 58T, 96, 130, 182T. **Stuart MacKay**: 56T, 112L, 128T, 140, 142T, 150BR, 154BR, 158B. **Mike McDowell**: 136T. **Dick McNeely**: 28T, B, 38N, 50N, 60, 88B, 90B, 118B, 120B, 122T, 206B, 242T, 244, 256, 308, 336T, 344B. **Tom Munson**: 118N, 226T, 352. **Dennis Paulson**: 64T, 146B, 180T, B, 208N, 208T, 256N. **Jim Pruske**: 60N, 68TL, BL, BR, 104T, 112BR, 126, 138TR, 150T, 184, 188, 198, 222T, B, 254B, 278, 306N, 310T, B, 342T, 344T, 346BR, 348T, B, 350B, 354B, 356T, BR, 358B, 368B, 372T, 374TR. **Jim Robertson**: 30T, 32T, 254T, 320B. **Jim Rosso**: 108N, 258N, 270N. **Robert Royse**: 38B, 42T, 44B, 54T, N, 66T, 74T, 76T, B, 134, 136B, 138BL, BR, 142B, TN, 146T, 148BL, 152T, B, 158T, 160TL, TR, B, 162B, 172N, 202T, 210B, 212B, 332T, 340, 342N, 346BL, 350T, 378BR. **Bart Rulon**: 32B, 34T, B, 36B, 56B, 66B, 82T, 94B, 104B, 144T, 150BL, 156, 162T, 272, 300, 304T, B, 338, 346TL, 362T, B, 372B. **Larry Sansone**: 264N. **Margaret St. Clair**: 48T, 70T, 72 T, 88T, 90T, 100N, 110N, 220L, 262T, 285, 294. **Michael Shepard**: 164T, B, 170T, B. **Brian Small**: 36T, 44T, 48B, 50T, 52B, 58T, 62T, B, 72B, 74B, 82B, 84T, B, 86T, 92T, B, 94T, 98, 100B, 116, 226B, 154TR, BL, 174, 178B, 190B, 200, 206T, 214T, 216N, 220R, 222N, 232, 240, 242B, 246, 248, 250, 266, 270, 276B, 282, 290, 298, 306T, 312T, B, 318B, 320N, 322T, B, 324N, 314, 316B, 326, 328T, B, 332B, 342B, 346TR, 354T, 358N, 366. **Patrick Sullivan**: 336B, 374TL. **Ruth Sullivan**: 182B, 210T, 378TL. **Hank Tseng**: 114B, T, 128B, 258. **Idie Ulsh**: 142BN, 186T. **George Vlahakis**: 114N. **Barry Wahl**: 40T, B, 106, 264, 286, 292, 306B, 316T, 378BL. **Brian Wheeler**: 120T, 122B, 226N, 230B, 210, 374BL, BR. **Cathy Wise**: 358T. **Jim Zipp**: 162N, 214B, 380TR. **William Zittrich**: front cover, 212T. **Tim Zurowski**: 46B, 148T, 380BR.

The success of this guide is the success of all those who have contributed to it. Their participation is sincerely appreciated.

Index/Checklist of Puget Sound Region Birds

Use this checklist to keep a record of the birds you have seen.
Bold numbers are for the main Species Account page.

Other Species Seen

_____

_____

_____

_____

_____

_____

About the Authors

BOB MORSE

Bob has seen over 830 species of birds in the United States and has written/published eleven books. With Christina Morse, they operate the R.W. Morse Company which publishes and sells regional bird guides.

TOM AVERSA

Co-author of *Birds of the Willamette Valley Region* and *Birds of Southwestern British Columbia*, studied the birds of the Northwest while working at Woodland Park Zoo in Seattle and serving on the Washington Bird Records Committee. He has recently relocated to Maine.

HAL OPPERMAN

Principal author of *A Birder's Guide to Washington* (American Birding Association) and co-author of *Birds of the Willamette Valley Region*, has lived in the Seattle area since 1967. He is past editor of the Washington Ornithological Society's journal, *Washington Birds*.